2 to 22 DAYS IN TEXAS

THE ITINERARY PLANNER

RICHARD HARRIS

D0395740

John Muir Publications
Santa Fe, New Mexico

Other JMP books by Richard Harris:
2 to 22 Days in Florida
2 to 22 Days in the Pacific Northwest
2 to 22 Days in the American Southwest
Unique California

Thanks to Mary Shapiro, Richard Polese, Joanna Hill, and the Lone Star Sierra Club for their suggestions, which have been incorporated into this itinerary. Special thanks to Carl and Ruth Harris for helping me leave Del Rio. And extra special thanks to Rita Guidi for her assistance in all aspects of researching earlier editions of this book.

John Muir Publications, P.O. Box 613, Santa Fe, NM 87504

ISSN 1068-3011
ISBN 1-56261-210-7

Cover photo Leo de Wys. Inc./Bob Thomason
Design Mary Shapiro
Maps Jim Wood
Typesetting Sarah Johansson
Printer Banta Company

Distributed to the book trade by
Publishers Group West
Emeryville, California

CONTENTS

2 to 22 Days in Texas

HOW TO USE THIS BOOK

Most folks think they know what Texas is like. Fast money and flamboyant politicians. Soap-opera ranch life. Oil derricks towering like the skyscrapers of Dallas. Expanses of mesquite and tumbleweeds where cowboys and beef on the hoof can range from morning until night without crossing a road. Wide-open highways that beckon you to rediscover the sheer joy of driving. All these are parts of Texas, but most folks think of Texas the way those blind men in the old fable would describe a longhorn bull.

Texas is big. It is larger in area than any European country except Russia. Its population is greater than any state except California and New York, yet vast areas of it remain almost uninhabited. It contains more miles of paved highway than any other state in the United States. To sample the best parts of Texas takes at least three weeks; to explore the whole state takes a lifetime.

2 to 22 Days in Texas presents a carefully planned and tested itinerary for a three-week self-guided tour that covers the state's major cities as well as its eastern forests, Gulf Coast beaches, the Mexican border, the western mountains, the Chihuahuan Desert, and three national parks. You can follow each day's step-by-step instructions to explore Texas from its eastern corner to its southern tip to its western extremity, spanning 900 miles from east to west and over 500 miles from north to south. The total driving distance on this itinerary is about 3,000 miles.

If you have less than three weeks to travel, any portion of the first 14 days of this itinerary can easily be adapted to accommodate your vacation schedule. To abbreviate the trip to less than two weeks, simply follow as many days of the itinerary as you wish and then head for San Antonio, centrally located within a few hours' drive of any point in Days 1 through 14 and a half-day's drive by interstate highway from the trip's Dallas/Fort Worth starting point. Allow sufficient time if you plan to travel into West Texas, where driving distances are greater. For visitors with more than three weeks to travel, the itinerary ends in El Paso, the westernmost point, where continuing to other parts of the American Southwest is as easy as returning to Dallas.

The itinerary is divided into 22 daily sections, containing:

1. A **suggested schedule** for each day's travel and sightseeing.

2. A detailed **travel route** for each driving segment of your trip.

3. **Sightseeing highlights** rated in order of importance: ▲▲▲Don't miss; ▲▲Try hard to see; and ▲See if you get a chance.

4. Selective **food, lodging,** and **camping** recommendations.

5. **Helpful hints** and historical insights—random tidbits that will enhance your trip.

6. User-friendly **maps** designed to show you what the road up ahead is really like.

When to Go

Most tourists explore Texas during the summer months when schools are out. This is strange, because summer is the season for tornadoes on the northern plains, hurricanes on the Gulf Coast, and extreme heat in all parts of the state. Tornadoes and hurricanes are not likely to coincide with your visit, but heat can be a big problem for summer travelers. High temperatures explain why so many of the major tourist destinations in Texas are beaches, lakes, and rivers.

The ideal times to travel Texas highways are spring (late February through May), when you'll find the whole state abloom with wildflowers, and fall (September through November), when Indian summer lingers long and autumn colors begin to blaze in the forests. The climate is comfortably warm during these months, and on weekdays you'll never run into tourist crowds.

According to an old saying, Texas has two seasons: summer and January. Even in January, average temperatures are warm enough for camping. Except in the Panhandle and the mountains of West Texas, snow is almost unheard of. But in January and, less predictably, December and

February, arctic cold fronts called "northers" can blow into the state without much warning, dropping the thermometer from the 70s to way below freezing in a few hours. If you are camping on a winter trip, be prepared to retreat to a hotel or motel when cold weather suddenly sets in. Or, better yet, take a hint from the many "winter Texans" who migrate by RV and focus your winter travel plans on subtropical southern areas—South Padre Island, the Rio Grande Valley, Del Rio, and Big Bend National Park.

Suggested Schedules and Sightseeing Highlights
This book describes more sightseeing highlights than can be visited easily in a three-week trip. I've included extras to provide you with the necessary information to tailor the itinerary to your own interests by selecting from possibilities that range from wilderness to shopping malls, museums to beach resorts, dude ranches to border crossings, historical sites to university campuses. The suggested schedule at the beginning of each day presents a plan for visiting the area's key sights. Adapt the plan to make it your own by skipping scheduled stops in favor of other sightseeing highlights that sound good to you, or spend an extra day in the region and see everything. It's your vacation, and this book's purpose is not to restrict you but to free you.

The sightseeing highlights in this book are not all the places one could visit along this route, just the best. I've picked each one because it is special in some way. For example, every Texas city of any size has an art museum, and many of them are excellent, but I've chosen to include Fort Worth's as *the* must-see art museum complex in Texas for the reasons stated in Day 1. If you're a connoisseur of art museums, you can find others on your own in Houston, San Antonio, Austin, and elsewhere by looking in the Yellow Pages. Similarly, though most Texas cities have zoos, the only one I've included is the Gladys Porter Zoo in Brownsville, one of the ten best in the nation. In all cases, I've tried to limit my suggestions to sightseeing highlights that are uniquely Texan—or, just plain unique.

Food

Eating is as essential to a total Texas experience as sightseeing is. The restaurants I suggest are those I've tried
personally and liked, as well as some that have been
recommended to me by others whose opinions I trust in
such matters. You'll discover other eating places just as
good in your travels, such as seafood shacks on the waterfront and nameless little barbecue places. Sightsee with
your tastebuds. There's no reason to settle for brandname
hamburger joints on this trip.

Texas has a wide variety of regional foods, from shrimp
along the Gulf Coast to Tex-Mex food on the border, and
in these pages I'll describe them for you. Traditional Texas
dishes such as chili and chicken-fried steak can be found
throughout the state. Perhaps the most Texan of cuisines is
barbecue, a word that means different things in different
parts of the state. In East Texas, barbecue may mean ribs
painted with a piquant sauce. In the north, it's a thick slab
of beef served without sauce. In the south, it's strips of
beef in chili sauce. And in the Hill Country, it's brisket and
German sausage in a sweet sauce.

The one common denominator in Texas barbecue is
mesquite, the state weed. This pretty, ornamental shrub
has run rampant across ranchlands ever since landowners
eliminated prairie dogs, who used to control mesquite
growth by nibbling on the roots. Inedible and impossible
to ride a horse through, mesquite has become such a problem that the state spends over a million dollars a year on
efforts to get rid of it. The result is huge piles of uprooted
mesquite, the only possible use for which is as an aromatic
cooking wood many people consider superior to hickory.
So barbecuing over mesquite is more than just a regional
luxury. It's practically a patriotic duty, and a tasty one at
that. Try it often.

Lodging

In most parts of Texas, you're never very far from an ordinary motel along the highway. The accommodations I've
included in this book, in all price ranges, offer something
special. Here you'll find suburban bed and breakfasts

where talking with the hosts can enhance your visit with fresh insights and local viewpoints. You'll also find elegantly restored historic hotels, often with room rates no higher than big-chain businessmen's hotels in the same locality, as well as picturesque park lodges. In West Texas, the lodgings I suggest are practically the only ones that exist, but each of them is special, too. Even if you're camping on this trip, plan to take a break and enjoy a little luxury every few days.

Camping

My recommendations include very few commercial RV campgrounds, because the Texas state park system provides full-hookup campsites in nearly 100 scenic locations throughout the state. Camping fees in the public campgrounds I suggest are lower than you'd find in private RV parks, and you won't find prettier spots at any price.

Visiting Mexico

U.S. and Canadian citizens do not need tourist cards, passports, or other documents to visit Juárez for short stays. If you wish to stay longer than 72 hours or travel farther than 18 miles south of the border, you will have to go through the formality of obtaining a tourist card and motor vehicle permit. Citizens of nations other than the United States or Canada must bring their passports. You will not be stopped by Mexican customs or immigration officials when crossing the bridge into Ciudad Juárez, but you will have to clear customs when returning to the United States side of the river. Customs checks are usually cursory for pedestrians but can be thorough and time-consuming for those in motor vehicles. Besides items that are illegal in the United States (narcotic drugs and switchblade knives, for example), U.S. Customs laws prohibit you from bringing back meats, fresh fruits or vegetables, or birds, animals, or plants. Food items you can bring back include bakery, candy, and nonperishable packaged foods. Tequila, mescal, and liqueurs such as Kahlua cost much less south of the border, even considering the 50-cent-a-bottle Texas alcoholic beverage tax you'll pay upon reentering the

United States; you can only bring back one liter of liquor per person per trip.

Mexican auto insurance is essential if you plan to drive your vehicle over the border. United States auto insurance does not cover you in Mexico. Having an uninsured accident, no matter how minor, is a criminal offense in Mexico, meaning that you will stay in jail until you pay for the damage. Mexican auto insurance is sold conspicuously at all border crossings. It costs around $10 for single-day coverage. For short visits, it's simpler to walk across the border. Tourist zones and public marketplaces are generally near the international pedestrian bridges, and you can do quite a bit of traveling around Mexican border cities by taxi at about the same amount you'd pay for car insurance. Taxi fares are negotiable, so be sure to agree on the price before getting into a taxicab. Your willingness to compare around the taxi stand for the lowest bidder will bring taxi fares down remarkably.

Recommended Reading

The history and cultures of Texas are unique, and reading a few books before you start out—or en route—will add to your understanding and enjoyment of this trip.

The ultimate popular book about Texas is *Texas* by James A. Michener (New York: Random House, 1985), a 1,300-page dramatized history of the state from Spanish colonial times to the present day that will keep you occupied for many a long winter evening.

Though Texas has rarely been mentioned in the same breath with literature, there are generally considered to be three "classic" Texas writers. The most popular is J. Frank Dobie, whose works include *Tongues of the Monte* (Boston: Little Brown, 1935) and *A Guide to the Life and Literature of the Southwest* (Austin: University of Texas Press, 1943). The others are Walter Prescott Webb, author of *The Texas Rangers* (Boston: Houghton Mifflin, 1935) and *The Great Frontier* (Boston: Houghton Mifflin, 1952), and Roy Bedichek, author of *Adventures with a Texas Naturalist* (New York: Doubleday, 1947). All of these books are available in reprints from the University of Texas Press.

Larry McMurtry might be the finest Texan novelist writing today. Most of his books—*Some Can Whistle, Lonesome Dove, Terms of Endearment,* and *Texasville,* among them—explore various aspects of Texas life, urban and rural, past and present. An often-overlooked little McMurtry book that is worth searching for is *In a Narrow Grave: Essays on Texas* (New York: Simon & Schuster, 1968), which includes among other delights a long, humorous account of a driving trip across the state.

When visiting your bookstore, order a copy of *The Roads of Texas,* an atlas containing 148 large pages of detailed sectional maps that show you where all those roads not taken go. It's the most useful tool I know for exploring Texas off the beaten path.

DAY 1   Arriving in the Dallas/Fort Worth Metroplex, crossroads of four interstate highways and site of the nation's largest hub airport, begin your explorations in the most quintessentially "Texan" of Texas cities, Fort Worth. Today's highlights include a walking tour of the Stockyards Historic District (once the world's largest livestock market), three distinctively Texan art museums in the city's Cultural District, and perhaps an evening rodeo.

DAY 2   This plan for seeing Dallas in a day includes the John F. Kennedy Memorial and assassination site, the Sixth Floor Exhibit in the former Texas School Book Depository, the West End Historic District, Neiman Marcus, and a drive through the Texas Rich neighborhood along Turtle Creek to stroll through the lobby of one of the most elegant hotels in America.

DAY 3   A drive through the pineywoods country of East Texas presents opportunities to ride the Texas State Railroad, visit Mission Tejas (the first Spanish mission in Texas) and Caddoan Mounds (remains of an ancient Indian civilization), and take a hike in Davy Crockett National Forest.

DAY 4   Complete your East Texas journey with visits to two very different natural ecosystems. Big Thicket, a UNESCO Man and Biosphere Reserve, protects the last ancient forest wilderness in Texas. On your way through Big Thicket, stop to visit the state's only Indian reservation, the home of the Alabama and Coushatta tribes. Then continue south to the Gulf of Mexico and drive the road along beaches and wetland wildlife refuges that are home to wading birds and alligators. The day ends with a ferry trip to Galveston.

DAY 5   Galveston was the major seaport in nineteenth-century Texas until a hurricane all but wiped it off the map. Today this seashore resort city offers 32 miles of beach as well as an impressive array of restored historic mansions.

DAY 6   A day trip out of Galveston to Houston, the largest city in Texas, gives you a chance to visit the Lyndon B. Johnson Space Center. "Cruise the Loop" for an overview of skyscraper islands in the only major American city that has no zoning laws. See one of the nation's most fabulously decorated mansions, an ultraexclusive shopping mall, and the original indoor football stadium.

DAY 7   Highlights of the drive down the coast from Galveston include Aransas National Wildlife Refuge, the winter home of the whooping crane. Today's journey ends at Padre Island National Seashore, a pristine 50-mile stretch of wilderness beach.

DAY 8   After a morning of swimming or beachcombing, continue south across the King Ranch, the world's largest. Your destination, near the southern tip of Texas, is South Padre Island, a palm-studded, almost tropical resort area that resembles South Florida more than it does the other end of the island.

DAY 9   Winter never reaches the southern tip of Texas where citrus growers, retirees, and "snowbirds" populate friendly little cities such as Brownsville, Harlingen, and McAllen. Take a back-road drive through the farmlands along the Rio Grande. You may want to make an excursion across the border to Matamoros, Mexico.

DAY 10   Follow the Rio Grande all the way to Laredo, the pretty, historic, bicultural town that was, for two years in the 1840s, the capital of an independent nation, the Republic of the Rio Grande. After exploring the Texan and Mexican sides of Laredo, get on the interstate and drive north to San Antonio.

DAY 11   Visit the Alamo, Texas's most sacred shrine, in the shadows of downtown skyscrapers. Then stroll along San Antonio's chic, unique River Walk. In the afternoon, visit one or more of the city's seventeenth-century Spanish missions.

DAY 12   In Austin, see the state capitol and the sprawling University of Texas campus, where the highlight is the Lyndon B. Johnson Library with its full-scale reproduction of the Oval Office and memorabilia of the Vietnam War, the Great Society, and the personal life of the controversial president whom many Texans consider their greatest twentieth-century hero. Spend the afternoon beside one of the beautiful lakes on the city's outskirts. In the evening, find out why Austin is the live music capital of the Southwest.

DAY 13   Begin your two-day exploration of the magnificently scenic Hill Country with a visit to the Lyndon B. Johnson Ranch and then visit nearby Pedernales Falls State Park. Spend the evening in the "Texas Dutch" community of Fredericksburg.

DAY 14   Exploring deeper into the Hill Country, you'll discover tiny German villages that seem not to have left the nineteenth century yet and have an opportunity to hike into the wilderness at Lost Maples State Natural Area. Later in the day, en route back to the Rio Grande, you may wish to visit the set of the John Wayne movie version of *The Alamo*—more realistic than the real thing.

DAY 15   At the junction of the Rio Grande and Pecos rivers, Amistad International Reservoir is the largest lake in Texas. Rent a boat and relax today or explore historic downtown Del Rio and cross the river via the international bridge to Ciudad Acuña, Mexico.

DAY 16   Visit Seminole Canyon, site of caves impressively muraled with Indian pictographs that have survived for 8,000 years. See the saloon/courtroom of Judge Roy Bean in Langtry and learn how "Law West of the Pecos"

worked. Then drive through the emptiness and stark beauty of the Chihuahuan Desert to arrive late in the day at Big
Bend National Park.

DAY 17   This huge, mountainous park is one of the best-
kept secrets in the National Park System. Take a hike
around the circular rim of the Chisos Mountains. Tour the
park by car to visit the Rio Grande and its spectacular
gorges.

DAY 18   Explore West Texas. Take a day to discover
unusual places in the middle of nowhere, including historic Fort Davis and Davis Mountains State Park. The town
of Marfa has two claims to fame. One—the location for
the motion picture *Giant*—is gone without a trace. The
other—the unexplained mystery of the Marfa Lights—can
be seen most evenings.

DAY 19   Guadalupe Mountains and Carlsbad Caverns
national parks, almost contiguous, straddle the Texas/New
Mexico state line. Set aside the later part of your day for a
self-guided tour deep into Carlsbad Caverns.

DAY 20   This morning, take time for a hike into the
Guadalupe Mountains to discover charms hardly hinted at
from the road. On the way into El Paso, stop to visit the
great stone maze of Huecos Tanks.

DAY 21   Visit the Tigua Indian Pueblo and other El Paso
area attractions, including the Border Patrol Museum. Then
cross the border for marketplace shopping and spicy food
in Ciudad Juárez.

DAY 22   This itinerary leaves you at the westernmost
point in Texas, 600 empty miles from where you began.
You can close the loop, if you wish, by returning directly
to Dallas/Fort Worth in a very long, unavoidably dull day
of driving on the interstate. A more interesting possibility is
to continue northward into New Mexico and, if you wish
to return to Dallas, cross the Panhandle, the only area of

the state where the main itinerary does not take you. The main attraction is spectacular Palo Duro Canyon, the largest in Texas.

FORT WORTH

"Fort Worth," Will Rogers once quipped, "is where the West begins and Dallas peters out." Like the West itself, this 22-day itinerary begins in Fort Worth. Explore both sides of a unique city that has held onto its Western heritage and yet developed a taste for the finer things in life.

Suggested Schedule

10:30 a.m.	Visit the Stockyards Historic District. Stroll, shop, eat lunch.
1:00 p.m.	Drive to the Cultural District. Visit the Amon Carter Museum.
2:00 p.m.	Cross the street and see the Modern Art Museum.
3:00 p.m.	Visit the Kimbell Art Museum.
5:00 p.m.	Take a walk through the Botanic Gardens.
Evening	Eat a good steak dinner. Later, two-step to country-western music at a Stockyards District saloon. Spend the night in Fort Worth.

Getting Around the Metroplex

The metropolitan area of Dallas (pop. 1,000,000), Fort Worth (pop. 450,000), and the suburban municipalities such as Arlington, Irving, and Grand Prairie that sprawl between the two cities is called the Metroplex (total population 3,900,000). Both cities share Dallas-Fort Worth International Airport, midway between them via the Airport Freeway (TX 183). The largest airport in the United States, it is made up of several separate D-shaped terminals with no central waiting area. Shuttle buses connect the airport to downtown Fort Worth or downtown Dallas for $10 per person one-way. A cab ride from the airport to either city costs about $40 one-way. If you are arriving by air, it pays to rent a car at the airport even if you only use it to get to your hotel and pick up a long-term rental auto or RV tomorrow.

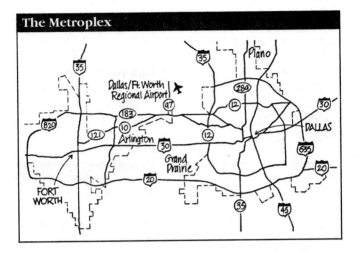

The Metroplex

The two cities have a confusing multitude of freeways. One or another of them is always near you. To keep track of where you are, visualize each interstate highway separately.

The east-west freeway to know is Interstate 30, which connects downtown Fort Worth and downtown Dallas. The simplest route between the two cities, it does not continue very far west of Fort Worth before merging with I-20; out of the east, it comes from Little Rock, Arkansas, where it merges with I-40. The other main east-west freeway, Interstate 20, connects the south part of Fort Worth's loop freeway (I-820, the Jim Wright Freeway) with the south part of Dallas's loop (I-635, the Lyndon Johnson Freeway). I-20 arrives out of the west as an offshoot of I-10 from El Paso, and out of the east from Atlanta, Georgia, by way of Jackson, Mississippi, and Shreveport, Louisiana.

The most important north-south freeway is I-35, which comes out of the north from Oklahoma City and continues south to Austin and San Antonio. I-35 forks into two freeways north of the Metroplex at Denton and reunites to the south near Hillsboro. I-35W goes to Fort Worth, while I-35E goes to Dallas. Each branch meets I-30 at its city's downtown area.

I-45 is the highway you'll want to take on Day 3 when leaving the Metroplex en route to the East Texas forests and the Houston area. It intersects I-30 and I-35E near downtown Dallas and can also be reached from Fort Worth by taking I-20 east to exit 473 on the extreme southern outskirts of Dallas.

Dallas and Fort Worth

Fort Worth and Dallas are two sides of the same coin—opposite, yet inseparable. Fort Worth was the area's commercial center in the early twentieth century, when it was the world's largest livestock market, the place every West Texas rancher went when he went to the big city. Dallas started as a seaport, until it was discovered that ships couldn't get there; instead, Dallas became a railroad shipping point and later a major crossroads where I-35, I-45, I-20, and I-30 merge, connecting the Metroplex with the rest of Texas and most other places as well. With oil companies, insurance companies, high-tech firms, and the fashion industry, not to mention the glamorous image created by its namesake television series, Dallas's economy has grown much faster than Fort Worth's in recent years. But never suggest in Fort Worth that the city is a suburb of Dallas. It ain't so. Dallas and Fort Worth are twin cities, separate but equal, one representing the modern, growth-oriented eastern half of Texas, the other the still-wild frontier that is the western half. Dallas is where Texans lose their drawls, the majority of residents come from other states, and more people carry briefcases than wear 10-gallon hats. Fort Worth remains a place where the police ride horses and a man can walk bowlegged into a saloon to recover from a bout with a buckin' bronco and not have to worry about cleaning off his boots first.

I recommend Fort Worth as the ideal starting point for a Texas get-acquainted tour because, more than any other city in the state, it both embodies Texas cowtown stereotypes and questions them. In the week that follows, you'll discover that a lot of Texas is not the land of cowboys and horses anymore. Later in the trip, you'll see that a lot of it is, too. Fort Worth has a downtown area of looming

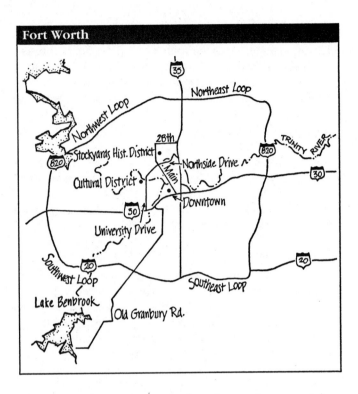

Fort Worth

skyscrapers, but I suggest that you bypass it on a quick visit and head for the Stockyards District instead. Tomorrow promises sufficient big-city sightseeing in downtown Dallas.

Sightseeing Highlights
▲▲▲**Stockyards Historic District**—The nation's second-largest national historic district, the Fort Worth Stockyards began as a rail terminal where cattle ranchers drove their herds for sale and shipment to the East. The elaborate storefronts and brick-cobbled streets date back to that era. During World War I, Fort Worth became the world's largest livestock market as the U.S. Army came here to buy horses and mules to take to Europe. Today, the ranching industry works differently, and most Texas cattle go to giant feedlots elsewhere to be fattened for slaughter. The livestock pens at the Fort Worth Stockyards

are empty now; even the smell is gone. But the saloons and cowtown streets remain to evoke a solidly authentic Old West atmosphere along N. Main Street and Exchange Avenue. To get there, take the 28th Street exit from Interstate 35 north of downtown.

This is one of the few historic districts in America which has not allowed itself to be gentrified. You won't find much in the way of fashion boutiques, art galleries, or frozen yogurt shops here. Instead, you'll find Western wear and saddle shops and the corniest souvenir establishments in Texas. Bring your sense of humor along. If you're in the market for a pair of Texas-shaped sunglasses, a longhorn ashtray, or a T-shirt that says, "I Bin to Hell, and TEXAS is Better!" you've come to the right place. If you'd like to get into the proper spirit for a journey around Texas by outfitting yourself in "Wranglers, Ropers, and a Resistol" (blue jeans, boots, and a cowboy hat), the Stockyards District is where you'll find the best selection.

Today, professional offices occupy most of the Spanish-style Livestock Exchange Building at 131 E. Exchange Avenue, but it also contains the North Fort Worth Historical Society Museum in suites 113 and 114, where exhibits recount earlier days in the Stockyards District. The free museum is open Monday through Friday from 9:30 a.m. to 4:00 p.m. Behind the Exchange Building is a livestock auction arena that is still in use. Cattle auctions are held every Monday at 10:00 a.m., and hog auctions every Monday and Tuesday at 9:00 a.m. The larger building just west of the Exchange Building is the Cowtown Coliseum. When it was built, it was the world's first indoor rodeo arena. Rodeos are held here every Saturday night at 8:00 p.m. from the beginning of April through Labor Day as well as at other times throughout the year, including Pioneer Days in late September and the Texas Championship Rodeo at the end of December. For current event information, stop in at the Fort Worth Visitor Information Center in front of the Coliseum, open daily during the summer months, Thursday through Monday the rest of the year, from 10:00 a.m. to 5:00 p.m.

▲▲**Cultural District**—Every Texas city has its museum

of art (locally pronounced "ort"). You could spend a
whole 22-day tour visiting them. Many Texas art museums
have impressive acquisition budgets, thanks to people
who have amassed fortunes in ranching, oil, or real estate
development and set out to prove that, contrary to popular belief, Texas really does have fine arts—all that money
can buy. I have selected those in Fort Worth's Cultural
District to include in this suggested itinerary because the
museums are small enough to tour comfortably in an
afternoon, collections are exceptional in quality, and
admission is free. The contrast with the gritty cowboyness
of the Stockyards District makes them extra special.

The Cultural District is about three miles from the
Stockyards District. From N. Main, turn west on Northside
Drive, which veers around to the south and becomes
University Drive. The three art museums are on Camp
Bowie Boulevard between University and Montgomery.
Look for the most visible Cultural District landmark, the
tower over the entrance to the nearby Will Rogers
Equestrian Center.

The **Amon Carter Museum** is generally considered to
be the finest public collection of American Western art
anywhere. Amon Carter was the founder and publisher of
the *Fort Worth Star-Telegram* newspaper back in the
1930s and 1940s and became the mayor of Fort Worth. It
is said that Carter disliked museums, but he loved the oil
paintings and bronze sculptures of western artists Frederic
Remington and Charles M. Russell and built an extensive
personal collection of their works. Finally, he endowed
this museum to share them with the public. The museum
also has works by most other famous western artists,
including paintings by Georgia O'Keeffe and photographs
by Ansel Adams and Eliot Porter. Temporary exhibitions
fill the second level. The museum is open Tuesday
through Saturday from 10:00 a.m. to 5:00 p.m., Sundays
12:00 noon to 5:30 p.m., closed Mondays. Free guided
tours are offered at 2:00 p.m.

The **Modern Art Museum of Fort Worth**, across Camp
Bowie Boulevard from the Amon Carter Museum, has
works by Pablo Picasso, Jackson Pollock, Mark Rothko,

and Andy Warhol, among others, in its permanent collection. It also shows temporary and traveling exhibitions. The Modern Art Museum is open Tuesday through Friday from 10:00 a.m. to 5:00 p.m., Saturdays from 11:00 a.m. to 5:00 p.m., Sundays 12:00 noon to 5:00 p.m., closed Mondays.

The **Kimbell Art Museum**, a block east of the Amon Carter Museum, is the legacy of oil tycoon Kay Kimbell. Though not very big, the museum has the second-largest acquisition budget of any art museum in the United States. Its director, Edmund Pillsbury, turned down a chance to become the director of London's National Gallery in order to stay in Fort Worth. The main hall of the museum exhibits antiquities and exotic works of sculpture and jewelry from places like ancient Greece and Egypt, pre-Columbian Mexico, India, and Africa. The wings on each side of the main hall show classical European and American paintings, including works by Goya, El Greco, Tintoretto, Rubens, Cézanne, and Monet. There's something distinctively Fort Worthian about the feel of this collection. For example, the Kimbell Museum must own more paintings of people cheating at cards than any other art museum on earth. For its most recent acquisition along these lines, a Caravaggio entitled *The Cardsharps*, the museum paid $15 million. The Kimbell Art Museum is open Tuesday through Friday from 10:00 a.m. to 5:00 p.m., Saturday 12:00 noon to 8:00 p.m., and Sunday from 12:00 noon to 5:00 p.m., closed Mondays.

▲▲**Botanic Gardens**—For a peaceful interlude at the end of the afternoon, take a stroll through these gardens just off University Drive south of the Cultural District. The acres include a rose garden and a $4 million conservatory for tropical flowers and plants. The grounds are open daily from 8:00 a.m. to 11:00 p.m.; the conservatory is open Monday through Friday from 10:00 a.m. to 9:00 p.m., Saturday 10:00 a.m. to 6:00 p.m. (4:00 p.m. in the winter), Sunday 1:00 to 6:00 p.m. (4:00 p.m. in the winter). Admission is $1 per adult. A separate admission ($2 per adult, $2.50 on weekends, and $1 per student ages 4 to 12) is charged at the adjoining Japanese garden with its pagoda, teahouse, and serenity. The Japanese garden is

open daily from 9:00 a.m. to 7:00 p.m. April to October,
Tuesday through Sunday 10:00 a.m. to 5:00 p.m. the rest
of the year.

▲**Sundance**—The newest historic restoration area in
Fort Worth lies downtown between Second and Fourth
streets, along Houston and Main streets. The area is
largely given over to restaurants and night clubs.

The highlight of a visit to the Sundance district is the
Sid Richardson Collection of Western Art at 309 Main
Street. If the Amon Carter Museum kindles enthusiasm for
the works of Frederic Remington and Charles Russell, you
can see 52 more paintings by these Old Western masters
at the private museum of a Fort Worth oil tycoon. Hours
are Tuesday and Wednesday from 10:00 a.m. to 5:00 p.m.,
Thursday and Friday 10:00 a.m. to 8:00 p.m., Saturday
from 11:00 a.m. to 8:00 p.m., and Sunday from 1:00 to
5:00 p.m., closed Mondays. Admission is free.

While you're in the area, notice the Richard Haas mural
depicting a cattle drive on the old Chisholm Trail. It's
down the street on the south wall of the Jetts Building,
400 Main Street. A main cattle drive trail once ran straight
through the middle of downtown Fort Worth.

▲**Cattleman's Museum**—The history of cattle ranching,
cattle drives, and cattle rustling is the subject of this private museum of the Southwestern Cattle Raisers'
Association. It is located at 1301 W. Seventh Street
between the Cultural District and downtown. Hours are
Monday through Friday from 8:30 a.m. to 4:30 p.m.,
closed Saturdays and Sundays. Admission is free.

Lodging

There is no reason to change accommodations during a
two-day visit to Fort Worth and Dallas. Compare this
section with the Dallas lodging section in Day 2. In
general, hotels and motels are less expensive in Fort
Worth than in Dallas. Availability is better in Dallas on
weekends and in Fort Worth during the week. The only
drawback to staying in Fort Worth is that you'll face more
rush-hour traffic hassles when leaving the Metroplex area
on the morning of Day 3.

Located in the heart of Fort Worth's Stockyards Historic District at the corner of Main and Exchange, the **Stockyards Hotel**, 109 E. Exchange Avenue, (817) 625-6425, was built in 1907 to provide luxury accommodations for visiting ranchers and livestock buyers. Refurbished in 1983, the hotel has a lobby full of western art and guest rooms decorated in Indian, cowboy, mountain-man, and Victorian motifs. Rooms for two start at just over $100, with suites such as the Bonnie and Clyde Suite, where the bank-robbing duo reputedly once lived it up, going for several hundred dollars a night. Still, the lower-priced rooms here are bargains for cattle baron elegance and a location convenient to the dining and nightlife of the Stockyards District; many rather regular businessmen's hotels in the Metroplex area cost more and offer much less for vacationers. The Stockyards Hotel has only 52 rooms, so advance reservations are a good idea, especially on rodeo nights.

Another historic accommodation in the Stockyards District, **Miss Molly's Hotel** at 109½ W. Exchange Avenue, on the second floor of the Commercial Building, used to be one of Forth Worth's most notorious bawdy houses. Today it operates as a bed and breakfast, with eight doubles in the $80 range as well as a Victorian suite. For reservations, call (817) 626-1522.

Ordinary motels are not easy to spot from highway approaches to Fort Worth. Good places to look for affordable places with vacancy signs are on University Drive south of the exit from I-30, near I-30 and TX 183 about 7 miles west of downtown, and near I-35 and US 81 south of downtown. All of these areas have plenty of motels with rooms in the $50-a-night range.

Camping

RV travelers and tent campers will find two campgrounds on the shore of Lake Benbrook, a municipal reservoir on the southwestern outskirts of Fort Worth. To get there, take Interstate 20, the freeway along the south side of the Dallas/Fort Worth Metroplex, heading west from I-35 or east from where the I-820 loop freeway joins I-20. Exit

I-20 at US 377 (Benbrook exit 429A) and drive 6 miles southwest to Park Road. Turn east there to reach **Holiday Park**, which has nearly 100 campsites, swimming, and nature trails. Sites cost $8, $10 with electrical hookup. The campground is open all year. The other campground is in **Mustang Park**. To reach it, continue on US 377 for another half mile past Park Road, then take Farm Road 1187 southeast for another 1½ miles, then Country Road 1125 east for about 2 miles. This is a smaller campground, about forty sites, with a beach. Camping fees at Mustang Park are the same as at Holiday Park. However, Mustang Park is only open from April through September.

Food

Beef—thick, juicy, mesquite-cooked slabs of it—is the special regional cuisine of Fort Worth. You'll find a selection of good steakhouses in the Stockyards District. Most are moderately priced and post their menus by the front door for your inspection. Try the **Cattlemen's Steak House**, in operation since 1947 at 258 N. Main, 624-3945, open Monday through Friday from 11:00 a.m. to 10:30 p.m., Saturday 4:30 to 10:30 p.m., Sunday 4:00 to 10:00 p.m. A little bit more upscale despite its name, **Booger Red's** in the Stockyards Hotel serves breakfast, lunch, and dinner in an atmosphere of Old West luxury, open daily from 6:30 a.m. to 10:00 p.m., Fridays and Saturdays until 11:00 p.m., 625-6427 ext. 71. For Tex-Mex fajitas and margaritas, go to **Los Vaqueros** at 2609 N. Main, 624-1511, open Monday through Thursday from 11:00 a.m. to 12:00 midnight, Saturday 12:00 noon to 12:00 midnight, and Sunday from 12:00 noon to 9:00 p.m. There is a **Spaghetti Warehouse** at 600 E. Exchange Avenue, 625-4171, past the rodeo arena and Exchange Building. The space it occupies once housed administrative offices of Swift & Company meat packers. The Spaghetti Warehouse is open Monday through Thursday from 11:00 a.m. to 11:00 p.m., Friday from 11:00 a.m. to 11:00 p.m., Saturday 12:00 noon to 11:00 p.m., and Sunday 12:00 noon to 10:00 p.m.

Nightlife

Billy Bob's Texas in the Stockyards District behind the
Coliseum at Rodeo Plaza and Stockyards Boulevard,
claims to be the world's largest honky-tonk. (Its only close
rival is Gilley's near Houston—see Day 6.) The 100,000-
square-foot complex has seating for 6,000, a giant dance
floor, and live music from top country and rock bands.
Also under the same roof are pool tables, pinball and
video games, restaurants, a gift shop, and mechanical bull
riding competitions on Friday and Saturday nights. Billy
Bob's Texas is open from 11:00 a.m. to 2:00 a.m. Call
589-1711 for current performance schedules and prices.

Other, smaller bars in the Stockyards District also have
live music and retain more of the authentic feel of Old
West saloons. On rodeo nights, expect these places to be
packed and very rowdy. The most famous historic drinking establishment in the district is the **White Elephant
Saloon** at 106 E. Exchange Avenue, 624-1887, which has
been a filming location for many Western movies and
television shows. Saloons along Exchange Avenue stay
open until 2:00 a.m. every night.

If your evening entertainment desires don't include
cowboys, a good alternate plan might be to visit the
Caravan of Dreams at 101 W. Second Street, one of
several popular nightclubs in the Sundance historic
district. The club features top-name jazz performers and
experimental theater performances. For current schedule
information, call 877-3000.

DALLAS

Two shootings made Dallas famous. The first was the assassination of President John F. Kennedy in 1963. The second, 16 years later, was the fictitious bullet that got J. R. Ewing, captured public imagination, and pushed the *Dallas* nighttime soap opera to the highest ratings in television history. Soon after *Dallas* faded from the airwaves and the show's exterior filming location, Southfork Ranch in the Metroplex's northern suburbs, closed its gates to the public, Oliver Stone's film *JFK* refocused attention on the assassination site, and the Sixth Floor became the city's biggest tourist attraction. Pay homage to Kennedy's memorial and check out the view from the window of the former Texas School Book Depository. You can explore the world of Texas millionaires by browsing in the original Neiman Marcus store or strolling through the lobby of the Mansion on Turtle Creek.

Suggested Schedule	
8:30 a.m.	Take your time eating breakfast and miss the rush hour.
9:30 a.m.	Drive from Fort Worth to Dallas.
10:15 a.m.	Visit the Kennedy Memorial in the Dallas County Historical Plaza.
11:00 a.m.	Take a walk through the skyscraper canyons of downtown Dallas.
1:00 p.m.	Lunch in Neiman Marcus or the West End Historic District.
2:00 p.m.	Visit the museums in Fair Park or, if you prefer, drive up Turtle Creek Boulevard to the Mansion.
Sunset	Watch it from the observation deck of Reunion Tower.
Evening	Return to your lodgings and prepare to head out on the road tomorrow morning.

Travel Route: Fort Worth to Dallas (35 miles one way)
Interstate 30 goes directly from downtown Fort Worth to downtown Dallas. Look for metered parking along Market Street south of the Dallas County Historical Plaza ·

Dallas

Dallas is a city of highly visible money and materialism but also of an overwhelmingly positive mental attitude, a fast-track energy, a solid conviction that everything is sure to keep getting bigger and better. Visionary dreams have a way of coming true in Dallas. Henry Ford built an automobile assembly line here way back in 1913. A few years later, Blue Cross and Blue Shield originated the concept of health insurance here. Also in Dallas, the family-owned Southland Ice Company parlayed its holdings into a nationwide empire of 7-Eleven convenience stores, and Texas Instruments researchers revolutionized the electronics world by inventing the microchip. Today, Dallas continues to enjoy rapid economic growth, and its new business start-up rate ranks highest of any city in the nation.

State law used to require every insurance company doing business in Texas to keep a certain percentage of its assets in Texas banks or investments. It was this insurance money, as much as the region's fabled oil and cotton wealth, that built the skyscrapers of downtown Dallas. Over 200 insurance companies and 125 oil-related corporations are headquartered in these buildings. Sightseers who meander through the glass and concrete canyons find themselves amid a populace dressed in conservative business garb and carrying briefcases. The talk is peppered with phrases like financial statement, takeover bid, window of opportunity, and bottom line. Cowboy boots, Levis, and wide-brimmed hats are rarely seen in these parts.

Fashion is a key industry in Dallas, and the reason is cotton. Grown in the farmlands that surround the Metroplex, cotton is woven into textiles here and sewn into clothing to be exported around the world. Wholesale buyers descend on the 1.8-million-square-foot Dallas Apparel Mart each season to view the latest offerings displayed in 351 glass-enclosed exhibit suites, the largest clothing trade show on earth.

True, the Dallas economy had a few dents following the Texas oil bust of the mid-1980s and crises in financial institutions across the state. Only one Dallas bank remains locally owned today. Neiman Marcus, too, has come under non-Texan ownership, and even the Dallas Cowboys football team has been sold to a tycoon from Arkansas. What all this really proves, Dallasites insist, is that theirs has become a world-class city.

Sightseeing Highlights
▲▲**Dallas County Historical Plaza**—In 1841, founder John Neely Bryan built his small log cabin on a site within walking distance of modern-day downtown Dallas because he thought it was the natural place to establish a seaport. Bryan mistakenly believed that riverboats could maneuver 300 miles up the Trinity River from the Gulf of Mexico to deliver factory-made goods in trade for Texas beef and cotton. A steamboat actually did make it up the river to Dallas—once—for a $15,000 reward. Soon afterward, enthusiastic Dallas city fathers built their own steamboat, but it sank before reaching the sea. Bryan's vision finally paid off, though, as he lived to see Dallas become a major railhead in the 1870s. Today, four interstate highways meet just a stone's throw from Bryan's original homestead.

You can see John Neely Bryan's house, or at least a similar old log pioneer cabin dedicated to his memory, in the Dallas County Historical Plaza, located on the south-west edge of downtown at Main and Market streets. Nearby, gargoyles leer from the cornerstones of the Old Red Courthouse, the most ponderous edifice in the city back in 1890 when it was built, now a quaint sandstone relic in the shadows of skyscrapers.

The third structure on the plaza is the one place all Dallas visitors go out of their way to see. Some study it with puzzled expressions, for the empty black pedestal or altar surrounded by high white walls is very plain, and the interpretive plaque is ambiguous. Knowing that it was conceived as a cenotaph, or empty tomb, somehow fails to

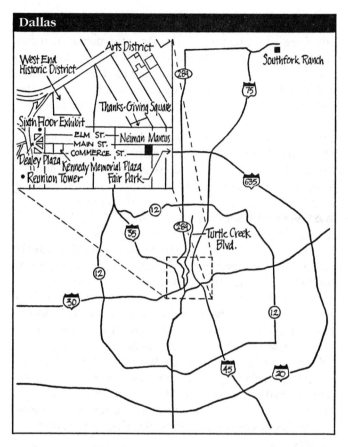

Dallas

- West End Historic District
- Arts District
- Southfork Ranch
- Thanks-Giving Square
- Sixth Floor Exhibit
- ELM ST.
- MAIN ST.
- COMMERCE ST.
- Neiman Marcus
- Dealey Plaza
- Kennedy Memorial Plaza
- Reunion Tower
- Fair Park
- Turtle Creek Blvd.

explain it. Zenlike, the structure invites visitors to bring their own meanings. It is the John F. Kennedy Memorial, an austere and silent reminder of the darkest hour in Dallas history.

▲▲▲**Dealey Plaza** and **The Sixth Floor**—The spot where the assassination bullets struck President Kennedy is a block north and two blocks west of the memorial, on Elm Street at the narrow end of Dealey Plaza. There is a small historical marker.

Nearby, on the corner of Elm and Houston streets, the former Texas School Book Depository still stands, and the sixth-floor window from which the shots were fired looks just like it did on television. In 1989, the Dallas County government, which now uses the building as administrative office space, opened the sixth floor to the public. You can visit the exhibit, called simply the Sixth Floor, to view films and displays on the assassination and the Kennedy legacy, look out the window at Dealey Plaza, and sense anew the reality of an event that changed America forever. Memory books, in which visitors are invited to write their feelings and remembrances, give history a deeply personal touch. The Sixth Floor is open daily from 10:00 a.m. to 6:00 p.m. (until 7:00 p.m. on Saturdays). Admission is $4 per adult, $3 for senior citizens, and $2 for students 6 to 18. Self-guided audio cassette tours cost an additional $2.

▲▲**West End Historic District**—More old brick ware-houses have been renovated to create the West End Historic District. Ask whether anything of historical significance ever happened in this district, and the response may be, "Why, uh, sure. They filmed some scenes for the *Dallas* TV show right over there." Whether truly historic or just old in a downtown area that otherwise looks sparkling new and often futuristic, the West End Historic District boasts some of Dallas's best restaurants and clubs. The centerpiece of the district is the West End Marketplace, a lively five-level complex of cute shops, video games, and international fast-food stands. One shop has what is probably the world's largest retail inventory of Kennedy assassination theories as set forth in books, tapes, maps, and posters.

▲**Thanks-Giving Square**—Exploring the city center can lead to unexpected surprises. Thanks-Giving Square, for example, was seemingly designed as a whimsical counterpoint to the John F. Kennedy Memorial by the same architects. On the "square," actually a triangular park between Pacific Avenue, Ervay, and Bryan, lawns and walkways slant at crazy angles down to a pool fed by manmade waterfalls. The interfaith Chapel of Thanksgiving, its ceiling a twisting spiral of stained glass, hints at the creators' original intent: to make an oasis of serenity for quiet contemplation secluded from the big-city hustle and bustle that surround it. In fact, Thanks-Giving Square has become one of the busiest places in downtown Dallas, a village green on a grand scale where office workers, retired folks, skate-boarders in punk rock garb, and fashion models all come to mingle. Especially during weekday lunch hour, there is no better place to people-watch in this part of Texas. The chapel also contains an exhibit tracing the history of Thanksgiving holiday observances in the United States. The square is open Monday through Friday from 9:00 a.m. to 5:00 p.m., Saturday and Sunday from 1:00 to 5:00 p.m. Admission is free.

Thanks-Giving Square is also a convenient starting point to explore the 3-mile network of underground walkways that honeycombs this part of downtown, connecting 23 major buildings beneath the streets. This "People Tunnel" serves a practical purpose, for Dallas weather is windier than Chicago and rainier than Seattle, and daytime temper-atures in the summer months frequently top 100 degrees. Still, many residents cite the climate as a key reason they live in Dallas: it hardly ever freezes.

▲▲**Neiman Marcus**—Three blocks south of Thanks-Giving Square at 1618 Main Street is Neiman Marcus, the store whose name has been synonymous with Texas-style elegance ever since 1907, when Carrie Marcus Neiman, her husband, and her brother joined forces to start a depart-ment store that would surpass any in New York City or Paris. For generations, tradition has dictated that any Texan who strikes it rich out in the vast, lonely oilfields to the west should immediately head for Neiman Marcus in Dallas to spend as much as possible of that newfound wealth.

Neiman Marcus looks unimpressive from the sidewalk, a rather plain building dwarfed by the city, and even inside each of its six stories feels small and intimate as depart-ment stores go—but oh, my, the merchandise (and the price tags)! Although the store has stiff competition in today's Dallas from branches of Saks Fifth Avenue, Macy's, Tiffany's, Bloomingdale's, and Marshall Field's, to name just a few well-known occupants of the city's 630 retail malls, Neiman Marcus holds a special place in the hearts of Texas shoppers. To find out why, visit the downtown store during Neiman Marcus Fortnight, a lavish spectacle of international arts and crafts, food and drink, antiques, and haute couture which coincides with the state fair during the last three weeks of October. The invitation-only Fortnight opening gala ranks among the most important events of the Dallas social season. At the other end of the spectrum are the semiannual Last Call sales Neiman Marcus stages in late January and late July, when every item in the store is marked down so far that people who do not own a single oil well can often find something priced within their budget.

Neiman Marcus is open Monday through Saturday from 10:00 a.m. to 5:30 p.m.

▲**Arts District**—"Dallas for culture, Fort Worth for fun" was a common saying in earlier times. Since then Fort Worth has gotten itself some culture, too, as you saw yesterday, and Dallasites have learned how to have fun, but Dallas remains peerless in the region for its cosmopolitan arts scene, now focused in the Arts District on the eastern edge of downtown. The centerpiece of the district is a massive stone cube of a building from which huge atrium windows seem to stretch groundward in sweeping curves. The **Morton H. Myerson Symphony Center** opened in 1989 as the new home of the Dallas Symphony Orchestra. Designed by I. M. Pei, the center cost $81 million to build and seats an audience of over 2,000 in five tiers. The symphony orchestra is one of the nation's largest and best endowed, with an annual operating budget that exceeds $10 million.

The other distinctive limestone and glass edifice in the Arts District is the **Dallas Art Museum**. Opened in 1984, the museum doubled its collection in 1985 with its acquisition of the Reves Collection, which now fills six second-floor rooms modeled after a French villa with Cézannes and Picassos, medieval furniture, a handful of paintings by Sir Winston Churchill, and a thousand other delights for the eye. The museum's collection of pre-Columbian art is also renowned. The museum is open Tuesday through Friday from 10:00 a.m. to 4:00 p.m., Saturday and Sunday from 11:00 a.m. to 5:00 p.m. Admission to the museum is free; there is a charge of $3 per adult, $2 for students and seniors, and $1 for children ages 1 to 11, to visit the Reves Collection. The museum is also open—and admission to the Reves Collection is free—every Thursday evening from 5:00 to 9:00 p.m.

First-time visitors following the route markers through downtown to the Arts District are sometimes disappointed to find that there are no art galleries or studios anywhere in sight. The artists' community is southeast of downtown, near Fair Park, in an old warehouse area known as Deep Ellum. The biggest concentration of studios there, L'Assemblage, is in the old Ford Motor Company assembly plant.

▲▲**State Fair Park**—The Texas State Fair, largest in the nation, draws 6 million visitors each October. Between fairs, the park off I-30 east of downtown is the site of a cluster of permanent attractions including the **Dallas Museum of Natural History** (open daily from 9:00 a.m. to 5:00 p.m., admission $5 for adults, $1 for children ages 3 to 11 and senior citizens), The **Science Place** (open daily from 9:30 a.m. to 5:30 p.m., admission $5.50 for adults, $2.50 for children ages 3 to 16 and senior citizens), the **Dallas Aquarium** (open daily from 9:00 a.m. to 4:30 p.m., admission $1 per person), and the **Dallas Civic Garden Center** (open Tuesday through Saturday from 10:00 a.m. to 5:00 p.m., Sunday 1:00 to 5:00 p.m., closed Monday, free). The most unusual of Fair Park's attractions, the Texas Hall of State (open Monday through Saturday) was built for the Texas centennial celebration in 1936. It contains the Museum of Texas History and the world's largest oil paintings.

▲**Turtle Creek Boulevard**—Running north from the downtown area, Turtle Creek Boulevard is one of the city's most exclusive addresses. A popular, pretty jogging trail follows the creek itself. The most elegant house on the block is The Mansion on Turtle Creek, 2821 Turtle Creek Boulevard, one of a series of Rosewood hotels conceived by Carolyn Hunt, whose father, oil speculator H. L. Hunt, started with $109 in his pocket and parlayed it into more money than television's J. R. Ewing ever dreamed of to become an archetypal Dallas personality. During his lifetime, Hunt was said to be the world's richest man. His

heirs have proven both philanthropic and discerning, and
their works are visible throughout Dallas—from Thanks-
Giving Tower and the Reunion Complex to the Bronco
Bowl and the Crescent Court. The Mansion, Rosewood's
magnificent restoration of a cotton baron's 143-room
Spanish-style house dating back to 1925, offers the ultimate
in gracious living on a four-acre estate five minutes from
downtown. Here the well-dressed sightseer can amble
nonchalantly through the opulent public rooms and enjoy
a vicarious sample of the lifestyle of the Texas Rich.

Also on Turtle Creek Boulevard, about eight blocks
north of the mansion, is the Dallas Theater Center, the
only theater Frank Lloyd Wright ever designed. Presen-
tations include Shakespearean, contemporary, and avant-
garde plays as well as shows for children. For current
schedule information, call 526-8857 or 526-8210. One of a
growing number of stage venues sprouting up in Dallas
to accommodate the city's 75 professional and amateur
theater groups, the Dallas Theater Center now has a second
location in the Arts District (922-0422).

▲**Reunion Tower**—To best appreciate the city's immensity, ride the elevator to the observation deck atop 52-story
Reunion Tower at 300 Reunion Boulevard on the southwest edge of the central business district around sundown.
In daylight, from this high vantage point, the far reaches of
the city are hidden by trees. Sunset makes the skyscrapers
glow magenta to appear as magical crystalline mountains
rising out of a forest. But as night settles and the lights
come on, dazzling illumination reaches all the way to the
distant horizon, sparking the realization that Dallas is much
larger than you imagined it to be. The observation deck is
open Sunday through Thursday from 10:00 a.m. to 10:00
p.m., Fridays and Saturdays from 10:00 a.m. to 12:00
midnight. The elevator ride to the top costs $2 for adults,
$1 for senior citizens and children under 12.

Lodging

Most accommodations in the Dallas area cater to business
travelers, not tourists. For those travelers to whom money
is no object, the city does have some of the finest luxury

hotels in the United States, notably the ultraelegant
Mansion on Turtle Creek (214-559-2100) north of downtown at 2821 Turtle Creek Boulevard. Equally plush and
steeped longer in tradition is the premier downtown hotel,
the **Adolphus** (1321 Commerce Street, 214-742-8200),
originally built by beer tycoon Adolphus Busch in 1912
and lavishly face lifted in 1981. The lobby, grand in scale,
features priceless art objects and the dark luster of walnut
panelling. Queen Elizabeth slept here, and so can you for
$215 to $260 a night.

But for the rest of us who blanch at the room rates of
such fabulous hostelries as these, the selection among
Dallas hotels and motels generally means a trade-off
between high prices, bland ambience, and inconvenient
location, making it more attractive to spend Metroplex
nights in Fort Worth instead.

Fortunately, there is an alternative to conventional
hotels in Dallas. Ruth Wilson operates **Bed & Breakfast
Texas Style**, the state's leading B&B reservation service,
representing about twenty establishments in the Dallas
area. Most are in suburban locations. Prices are lower than
you'd pay at a good hotel in the city—between $50 and
$60 at most places, up to $80 at a few historic homes.
Advance reservations are necessary. The reservation
service fees are paid by the host homes, so it costs no
more to book a room through this agency than to contact
the bed and breakfasts independently. Ms. Wilson also
books bed and breakfast accommodations across the state,
so you'll find it helpful to have your itinerary in mind
before you call her. Request a *Host Home Directory*
($3.50) from Bed & Breakfast Texas Style, 4224 W. Red
Bird Lane, Dallas, TX 75237, or call (214) 298-8586.

Camping
To reach **Lake Lewisville State Park**, drive north from
downtown Dallas on Interstate 35 for 21 miles and exit
eastbound on TX 121, then turn north on Farm Road 423
and follow the signs to the park. There are fifty lakeshore
campsites. Fees range from $9 to $12 per night.

On the opposite side of Lake Lewisville, closer to the

interstate, is **Oakland Park** with more than eighty camp-sites. About 23 miles north of Dallas, take the Lewisville exit from I-35 and follow the signs 3 miles east and 1 mile south to the park. Sites cost $8, with an extra $2 charge for electric hookup. Also near Lewisville but a little harder to find—4 miles west on Farm Road 407, then north on Chinn Chapel Road and east on Orchid Hill Lane—is **Pilot Knoll Campground** with 55 sites near the lake. Camping fees are the same as at Oakland Park.

All three campgrounds are open year-round.

Food

Dining at **The Mansion on Turtle Creek** (reservations are essential—call 559-2100) allows you to savor the luxurious ambience at leisure, as long as money is no object. The maitre d'hotel personally chooses which fortunate patrons will be seated in the main dining room; others are "exiled" to the veranda to enjoy the same cuisine—for example, antelope and wild rice salad followed by roast lamb with artichoke tarragon sauce. The dining room at the mansion serves breakfast daily from 7:00 to 10:30 a.m., lunch Monday through Friday from 12:00 noon to 2:30 p.m., brunch (about $25) on Saturday from 12:00 noon to 2:30 p.m. and Sunday from 11:00 a.m. to 2:30 p.m., dinner daily from 6:00 to 10:30 p.m., and late supper Monday through Thursday from 10:30 p.m. to 12:00 midnight. Men are required to wear coats and ties. Expect to spend at least $100 per person; coffee costs $6 a cup.

Downtown, you can mingle with the wealthy set somewhat more affordably at the **Zodiac Room** on the sixth floor in Neiman Marcus, 1618 Main Street, 741-6911. Models glide past in the very latest designer dresses and jewelry while you eat lunch. Some people claim that the fashion show atmosphere makes this a restaurant for women only; others know better. Neiman Marcus also has an espresso bar on the first floor.

For dinner, the classiest downtown restaurant is the opulent **French Room** in the Adolphus Hotel, 1321 Commerce Street, 742-8200. Amid huge potted plants under a dramatic vaulted ceiling hung with Italian crystal chandeliers and lavishly painted with baroque cherubs, the restaurant serves "neoclassical" cuisine (light, contemporary renditions of French dishes). The menu—in English—offers selections such as roasted yellowfish tuna loin, venison medallions served with sliced pheasant breast, and a Grand Marnier soufflé. Expect to pay about $50 per person.

Or sample the other end of the culinary spectrum at **Tolbert's Texas Chili Parlor** in Dallas Centre at the intersection of St. Paul and Bryan, 953-1353, with a second location in the West End at 1800 N. Market Street, 969-0310. I've found no other restaurant in the entire state that serves up better Texas-style chili (red, hot, no beans). For the timid, this reasonably priced downtown eatery also serves other, less spicy entrées. Tolbert's is open daily for lunch and dinner.

You'll find a multitude of other restaurants in the West End Historic District just north of the Dallas County Historical Plaza.

Nightlife

The famous, long-established nightclub zone in Dallas is Greenville Avenue northeast of downtown. The avenue is divided by Mockingbird Lane into chic **Upper Greenville** to the north and **Lower Greenville**, appealing to a younger crowd, to the south. Upper Greenville boasts the city's best comedy clubs.

The funky **Deep Ellum** district has an assortment of very informal dance clubs in old warehouses. Some are nameless. Top Deep Ellum night spots include **Club Clearview** (2806 Elm, 939-0006) and **Club Dada** (2720 Elm Street, 744-3232).

Much easier to locate on a short visit to Dallas is the West End Historic District downtown. The centerpiece of the district is **Dallas Alley** (988-9378), where under rainbow-hued neon arches nine separate nightspots and an outdoor concert stage serve up entertainment that ranges from piano bar sing-alongs and fifties rock 'n' roll to technopop dance music and the latest in video games.

EAST TEXAS FORESTS

The past blankets the pineywoods of East Texas like an Old South morning mist. On this first day of your leisurely, meandering journey between the two biggest urban areas in Texas, you'll travel on quiet secondary highways that wind past picture-perfect homesteads and through villages where you may feel that you're arriving slightly ahead of the 1990s. Along the route, little unpaved roads lead into the forest to old cemeteries marking the sites of early pioneer communities. Ride a nineteenth-century steam

Suggested Schedule	
8:30 a.m.	Depart the Dallas/Fort Worth area. If you stayed in Fort Worth last night, leave earlier to avoid morning rush-hour traffic. Or if the Texas State Railroad is not running (see Sightseeing Highlights for schedule), linger over breakfast and leave later.
11:00 a.m.	Ride the Texas State Railroad from Palestine to Rusk.
12:30 p.m.	Arrive at Rusk and enjoy a picnic lunch.
1:30 p.m.	Board the train for the return trip to Palestine.
3:00 p.m.	Back in Palestine, drive on to Davy Crockett National Forest.
4:00 p.m.	Visit either Mission Tejas State Historic Park or Caddoan Mounds State Historic Site. (Off-season travelers and others who don't take the train ride will have plenty of time to visit both.)
5:30 p.m.	Camp in the woods at Mission Tejas State Historic Park or by the lake at Ratcliff Recreation Area in Davy Crockett National Forest. Noncampers, drive on to Nacogdoches, Lufkin, or Woodville and check into accommodations there.

locomotive, visit the site of a seventeenth-century Spanish mission, or wander among the remnants of a thirteenth-century Native American town. Though both Dallas and Houston are just hours away, in time and distance the pineywoods seem much farther removed.

Travel Route: Dallas to Nacogdoches (181 miles)
If you spent last night in Fort Worth, get back on Interstate 30 and drive to Dallas again. Just after you pass the skyscrapers of downtown Dallas on your left, exit south-bound on Interstate 45, which promptly takes you out of the urban area.

I-45 is the main route between Texas's two largest cities. A word to the wise: drive 65 mph. More state police cruisers patrol for speeders here than on any other highway in the state, and the defense that everyone else was speeding too won't get you out of a ticket. If you stayed on this fast freeway, the drive from Dallas to Houston would take about four hours, but I suggest a more scenic route that will take two days and leave you wishing you had more time to explore East Texas.

Follow I-45 south from Dallas for 53 miles to Corsicana. This town of 23,000 is best remembered for the day in 1897 when the well being dug to create a municipal water supply surprised everybody by gushing oil instead. Exit from the interstate on US 287 eastbound and drive 59 miles to Palestine.

To reach the Texas State Railroad, take US 84 east for 2 miles to the Palestine terminal in Rusk-Palestine State Park. After the train trip, drive back into town and rejoin US 287. Stay on US 287 to Grapeland, 24 miles south of Corsicana. At Grapeland, turn east on Farm Road 227 and drive 14 miles to the junction with TX 21 near Weches.

To visit Davy Crockett National Forest, take a jog to the right (south) at TX 21, then turn left and continue on Farm Road 227 through the forest for 11 miles to Ratcliff, then return to TX 21 by the same route. The entrance to Ratcliff Recreation Area (see Camping) is on your right from TX 7 a short distance west of the Ratcliff intersection.

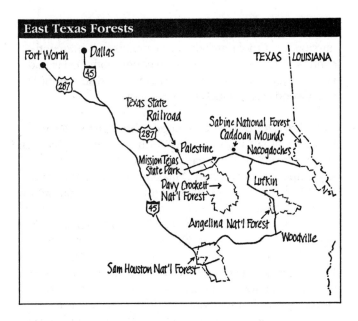

East Texas Forests

From the intersection of Farm Road 227 and TX 21, Mission Tejas State Historic Park is about 2 miles east on TX 21 (from Farm Road 227, turn left if you're coming from Grapeland or right if you're coming from Ratcliff). Continue on TX 21 for 7 more miles to Caddoan Mounds State Historic Park. From there, 31 more miles on TX 21 will bring you to Nacogdoches.

(Noncampers may choose to stay in Nacogdoches or, following the first part of tomorrow's travel route, continue down the road to Lufkin or Woodville.)

Sightseeing Highlights.
▲▲**Texas State Railroad**—Abandoned train tracks between Palestine and Rusk, 25 miles away, were given to the Texas Parks and Wildlife Department in 1972 to create Rusk-Palestine State Park, home to six steam locomotives from the late nineteenth century which are still in good running condition. Ride an antique passenger train through the forest, out of sight of modern development, and easily imagine yourself into an earlier era. The Rusk station has pleasant picnic sites, a small lake, and a children's playground.

The trains run during the summer months (last weekend in May through mid-August) Thursday through Monday, and in spring (mid-March through May) and fall (late August, September and October) on Saturday and Sunday only. The trains do not run during the winter months. A train leaves the Palestine depot at 11:00 a.m. (boarding begins at 10:15, and seating is first-come, first-served), arrives at Rusk at 12:30 p.m., allows you an hour to picnic there, and leaves at 1:30 p.m. to return to Palestine at 3:00 p.m. The round-trip fare is $15 for adults, $9 for children ages 3 to 12. Reservations are wise, though usually not essential. For reservations and current schedule information, call (214) 683-2561 or, within Texas, (800) 442-8951. You can make reservations at least ten days in advance by sending a deposit in the total amount of the ticket price (refundable upon cancellation at least 24 hours in advance) to Texas State Railroad, P.O. Box 39, Rusk, TX 75785. Reservations made less than ten days in advance do not require a deposit, but you must pick up the tickets at least an hour before departure or they will be sold to standby passengers.

(Another train leaves from Rusk, 30 miles east on TX 21, at 11:00 a.m. and follows the same schedule in reverse. If you can't make the 11:00 departure, you can catch the train from either station at 1:30 p.m. for a one-way trip—if you can talk a driving member of your party into skipping the train trip and picking you up at the other end. One-way fares are $10 for adults and $6 for children.)

▲**Davy Crockett National Forest**—To non-Texans, the name Davy Crockett conjures images of the pioneer woodsman who kilt him a b'ar when he was only three and popularized the coonskin cap. But in Texas, Davy Crockett's historical stature stems from events later in his life. At the age of 50, after losing his bid for reelection to the U.S. Congress, Crockett left his native Tennessee in disgust with a force of 12 volunteer militiamen to help defend Texas against the Mexican army. Although Crockett spent most of his brief days as a Texan within the walls of the besieged Alamo, his presence there symbolized United States support for Texas independence and won him the posthumous honor of having this national forest named after him.

Texans take their historical figures seriously and accord Crockett and his compatriots much greater importance than non-Texans like Abraham what's-his-name and that other fella who chopped down the cherry tree. A few years ago, historians revealed evidence that Davy Crockett had not died heroically fighting in the final assault on the Alamo but in fact had been taken prisoner and executed several days later. The seemingly innocuous discovery provoked such outrage that the historians received death threats; today their theory is buried deep in some musty Austin archive and never mentioned. Facts are fine, but Don't Mess with Texas.

Davy Crockett National Forest consists of "pineywoods" timberland that was deeded to the federal government for rehabilitation when all the usable timber had been cut. After the mid-1920s, no trees were felled for sixty years, and the second-growth loblolly, longleaf, and shortleaf pines had reached impressive size before logging resumed—over the protests of local residents—in the 1980s. Now fresh clearcuts are a common sight. Inholdings—tracts of private property within the national forest boundaries—occupy more than half the land in Davy Crockett National Forest, making much of the backwoods hard to reach.

The major hiking trail is the Four-C National Recreation Trail, which runs 10 miles between the Ratcliff Lake campground (see Camping) and the Neches Bluff campground (off TX 21 midway between Mission Tejas and Caddoan Mounds, on the opposite side of the highway). While the whole length of the Four-C Trail involves more hiking than most vacationers may wish to undertake, you can drive on unpaved forest roads (watch for the sign indicating the turnoff from Farm Road 227 halfway between Ratcliff and Weches) to Big Slough, where you'll find both the middle portion of the Four-C Trail and a network of old tram loop trails through one of the wildest parts of the forest. Boardwalks keep your feet dry above the soggy parts of the slough. Watch for white-tailed deer, which are common throughout this national forest; it is also the habitat of the endangered red cockaded woodpecker, whose presence has placed the Big Slough area off-limits to logging operations.

▲▲**Mission Tejas State Historic Park**—The first Spanish colonial settlement in Texas, Misión San Francisco de los Tejas was built in 1690 to Christianize the Tejas Indians and secure the Spanish claim to the region against French missionaries who were beginning to move west from Louisiana. No Tejas Indians survive today; the name of the tribe, later taken by the republic and state of Texas, actually meant "hello."

The log commemorative structure here is not the original mission, which was located a few miles to the west and used for only three years. This one was built by the Civilian Conservation Corps on what is believed to be the site of another mission used between 1716 and 1731. Also in the park is the Rice Family Log Home, one of the oldest surviving structures in East Texas (built between 1828 and 1838 as a stagecoach inn along the Old San Antonio Road, moved here from its original site 16 miles away in 1974). The best thing about this park is its lovely forest setting. Hiking trails, from 1 to 3 miles long, from easy and wheelchair-accessible to hilly and strenuous, start at the pretty little fishing pond and take you among tall pines and hardwoods. As a local fisherman told me sadly, "One time all of East Texas looked like this." The park is open daily from 8:00 a.m. to 10:00 p.m. The day-use fee is $2 per vehicle.

▲▲**Caddoan Mounds State Historic Site**—The Mound Builders were sophisticated Native Americans who built cities as far east as Florida and as far north as Ohio. Their civilization lasted for 2,500 years but suddenly vanished for unknown reasons about the time Columbus discovered America. Caddoan Mounds was the southwesternmost ceremonial center of this ancient, mysterious culture. Founded around A.D. 800, this settlement dominated the region for 500 years.

Two pyramidlike temple mounds and a burial mound are all that remain of this prehistoric city. The temple mounds were originally plastered with clay and had cane hut temples on top. The burial mound, first excavated in 1939-1941, yielded the stone, ceramic, and copper artifacts you can now see in the park museum. Equally interesting is the full-size replica of a Caddoan cane house, which was built by "experimental archaeologists" in 1981. Twenty-five feet in height, with 488 square feet of ground-floor living area, this hut took 11 weeks to build using tools and construction methods like those of the ancient Caddoans. Well, mostly. After each of the seven scientists had dug a support hole for one of the structural timbers, they gave up and rented a posthole digger for the other 19 holes.

Caddoan Mounds State Historic Site is open Wednesday through Sunday from 8:00 a.m. to 5:00 p.m., closed Monday and Tuesday. Admission is $2 per adult and $1 per child ages 6 to 12.

Food and Lodging
Rooms and meals can be found in Nacogdoches (pop. 31,000), 19 miles farther south in Lufkin (pop. 30,000), or 57 miles beyond there in Woodville (pop. 2,500).

In Nacogdoches, the **Tol Barret House** (Route 4, Box 9400, 569-1249) rents accommodations in an authentically furnished 1840s farmhouse, named after a former owner who was the first man ever to strike oil in Texas, as well as in the owners' restored 1820s pioneer home nearby. At this bed and breakfast, you cook your own breakfast; the gourmet fixin's are first-rate and often unusual. The rate for two people is $70 to $90. Reservations are essential.

Motels cluster around the junction of East Loop 224 and US 59. A good place to eat in Nacogdoches is **La Hacienda**, a Mexican restaurant in a converted house at 1411 North Street (564-6450). The top sights in Nacogdoches are all historic: the Old Stone Fort Museum, a replica of an eighteenth-century Spanish fort containing Indian artifacts, firearms, and such (on the Stephen F. Austin State University campus, open Tuesday through Saturday 9:00 a.m. to 5:00 p.m., Sunday 1:00 to 5:00 p.m., closed Monday, free admission); the Sterne-Hoya Home, where Sam Houston became a Catholic to qualify for land ownership in Texas (at the corner of Pilar and Lanana streets, open Monday through Saturday from 9:00 a.m. to 4:00 p.m., free admission); and Millard's Crossing, a pioneer village of nineteenth-century buildings (6020 North Street, open Monday through Saturday from 9:00 a.m. to 4:00 p.m., admission $3 per adult, $2 for children ages 5 to 12), all providing ample evidence that Nacogdoches is the oldest town in Texas.

Near Lufkin, country-style bed and breakfast accommodations are available at **Sweetwater Farm**, about $70 for two people. Reservations for a stay at the farm should be made through Bed and Breakfast Texas Style in Dallas, (214) 298-5433 or 298-8586.

Most motels in Lufkin are around the intersection of US 59 and Loop 287. A good place to eat in Lufkin is **Lemkes Wurst Haus** on TX 94, 1 mile west of Loop 287, serving reasonably priced German food and seafood, Monday through Saturday from 11:00 a.m. to 10:00 p.m., Sunday 5:00 to 10:00 p.m. Lufkin is the forestry capital of Texas, and the town's top sight is the Texas Forestry Museum (on TX 103 east, several blocks southwest of Loop 287, open 1:00 to 4:30 p.m. daily, admission by donation), where you can learn more than you ever wanted to know about how trees are cut down. Lufkin also has the Museum of East Texas (503 N. 2nd Street, open Tuesday through Friday from 10:00 a.m. to 5:00 p.m., Saturday and Sunday from 1:00 to 5:00 p.m., closed Mondays, free), with area history and art exhibits.

In Woodville, the finest (and only) lodging is the modern **Woodville Inn**, (409) 283-3741. It has a swimming pool, and a room for two costs under $60. While the inn has a restaurant, the most unusual place to eat in Woodville is the **Pickett House**, 283-3946, open during the spring and summer months daily from 11:00 a.m. to 8:00 p.m., Saturday 11:00 a.m. to 8:00 p.m., and Sunday 11:00 a.m. to 6:00 p.m. Country cooking is served boardinghouse-style in this converted turn-of-the-century school, all you can eat for $6 on weekdays, $7 on weekends. The Pickett House is located at the Heritage Village an open-air folk museum with nearly two dozen pioneer buildings (1 mile west of town on Highway 190, museum open daily from 9:00 a.m. to 5:00 p.m., until 6:30 p.m. during the summer months, admission $1.50 per adult and 75 cents per child). Also in Woodville is the Allan Shivers Museum (302 N. Charlton St., open Monday through Friday from 9:00 a.m. to 5:00 p.m., Saturdays from 10:00 a.m. to 2:00 p.m., $1 for adults, and 50 cents for children ages 5 to 17), the restored home of a former Texas governor.

Camping

The campground at **Mission Tejas State Historic Park** is my favorite in the area because of its beautiful piney-woods setting and hiking trails. Sites cost $6 per night, or $10 with electric hookup.

Another fine camping option is **Ratcliff Recreation Area**, which is on the shoreline of a fishing lake (motor-boats prohibited) and offers exceptionally spacious camp-sites for $8 per night, with a few higher-priced sites that have water and electric hookups. The part of the Four-C Hiking Trail near the campground, unfortunately, has recently suffered Texas chainsaw massacres.

Of the two campgrounds, Ratcliff is more likely to be crowded on weekends during the warm months. On weekday evenings, you'll find plenty of room at both campgrounds.

More about National Forests in Texas

Texas has four national forests, each within a two-hour drive of Nacogdoches and Lufkin. Together, they make up roughly half the public lands in the state. I've chosen to include only Davy Crockett National Forest in the main 22-day itinerary because of its proximity to other East Texas points of interest. For readers who have extra time and would like to spend it hiking, boating, or fishing in the pineywoods country, here is information on the other three national forests.

Angelina National Forest can be reached by taking US 69 from Lufkin 22 miles southeast to Zavalla, where secondary highways lead to all parts of the forest. The forest covers most of the 560-mile shoreline of Sam Rayburn Reservoir, named for the U.S. congressman from East Texas who served as speaker of the House of Representatives longer than any other congressman in history. The largest lake entirely within Texas (only Amistad Reservoir on the Mexican border is larger—see Day 15), it is a popular place for bass fishing. You need a Texas fishing license, available at any bait and tackle shop, to fish in the national forests. A dozen campgrounds, most of them operated by the Corps of Engineers, are located along the lake shore. Motorboats make all of these campgrounds noisy, but only during daylight hours. Hikers may prefer the campground at Boykin Springs Recreation Area (follow TX 63 for 8 miles southeast from Zavalla and turn right on Forest Road 313), which has a small natural lake and the trailhead for the 6-mile (each way) Sawmill Hiking Trail. Angelina National Forest is named for a legendary Indian woman who befriended early Spanish and French missionaries in the area; she is also the only woman to have a county in Texas named after her.

Sabine National Forest is reached by driving 57 miles east of Nacogdoches on TX 21 or 53 miles east of Lufkin on TX 103. The forest lines the western shore of Toledo Bend Reservoir on the Sabine River, which marks the Texas/Louisiana state line. There are no recreational hiking trails in Sabine National Forest, though many timber roads there are used by hikers. On the lakeshore are five national forest campgrounds, and numerous inholders operate fishing resorts and marinas.

Sam Houston National Forest, south of the other three national forests, can be reached by driving 77 miles south from Lufkin to Cleveland on US 59 or 68 miles north from Houston to Huntsville. On the outskirts of Cleveland and Huntsville are the beginning and end of the 140-mile Lone Star Trail, the longest public hiking trail in Texas, which was established in 1968 through the efforts of the Sierra Club. If the entire length of this trail (which takes about a week to hike one-way) sounds like too much, you can hike a portion of it through the unspoiled Big Creek Scenic Area by exiting US 59 westbound from

Shepherd, 12 miles north of Cleveland, driving about 5
miles, turning north on Forest Road 221, and driving
about a mile to the parking area. The forest was named,
of course, for the "George Washington" of Texas, the
revolutionary leader who became the first president of the
Republic of Texas but later fell from popularity because of
drinking problems and antislavery sentiments.

The best times to explore Texas national forests are
spring and fall. Be careful of deer hunting season, though.
National forests are practically the only public lands in the
state where hunting is allowed. Affluent hunters lease
game rights on private ranches, but firearms enthusiasts of
modest means generally head for the national forests to
blast away at wildlife, making them hazardous places to
stroll during November and December.

Maps of all four national forests, as well as brochures
describing hiking trails and recreation areas, are available
on request from Forest Supervisor, Federal Building, 701 N.
First Street, Lufkin, TX 75901.

THE BIG THICKET AND THE NORTH COAST

The last remaining wilderness in East Texas is this morning's destination. After visiting the few Native Americans who live in the Big Thicket and strolling down a trail that tantalizes you with a brief taste of what the primeval forests were like, head south to drive a long, wide open road along a mostly vacant, wildlife-rich stretch of the Texas coast, ending with a ferry ride to Galveston, the state's busiest beach resort.

Suggested Schedule

9:00 a.m.	Leave Nacogdoches (earlier if you camped in one of yesterday's suggested campgrounds, later if you stayed in Lufkin or Woodville last night).
10:30 a.m.	Visit the Alabama-Coushatta Indian Reservation. Take a tour into the Big Thicket or see the Indian village and dance performance.
12:00 noon	Lunch at the restaurant in the Indian village.
12:30 p.m.	Drive to the Big Thicket Visitors Center.
1:30 p.m.	Walk the nature trail near the visitors center.
2:30 p.m.	Drive on through Beaumont to Port Arthur.
3:30 p.m.	From Port Arthur, drive to the Gulf Coast. Follow the coastline all the way to the tip of the Bolivar Peninsula.
5:30 p.m.	Take the ferry to Galveston. Check into your accommodations in Galveston for a three-night stay or camp for the night a little farther down the coast at Galveston Island State Park.

Travel Route: Nacogdoches to Galveston (267 miles)
From Nacogdoches, drive south on US 59 for 19 miles to
Lufkin. Watching carefully for the exit from the freeway
loop that goes around (and around and around) Lufkin,
exit onto US 69 southbound and go 48 miles through
Huntington and Zavalla to Woodville. Turn west (left) at
Woodville on US 190 and go about 20 miles to the
Alabama-Coushatta village (signs say "Indian Village").

After visiting the Indian village, continue west on US 90
for a few miles to the intersection with FR 1276. Turn
south (left) on FR 1276 and drive 14 miles, which takes
you through the Big Sandy Creek unit of Big Thicket
National Preserve. Then turn east (left) on FR 943 and go
21 miles, then north (left) on US 69/287 for 2 miles, then
east (right) on FR 420 for 4 miles to the Big Thicket
Visitors Center.

After retracing your 4-mile route from the visitors center
to US 69/287, turn south (left) and drive 23 miles to
Lumberton, where the route joins US 96. Continue on US
69/287/96 for 27 miles through Beaumont (pop. 125,000,
difficult if you arrive during the 4:00 to 6:00 evening rush
hour), where the route merges with Interstate 10, then
separates two exits later. Stay on US 69/287/96 southbound to Port Arthur (pop. 65,000), another 17 miles.

Just north of downtown Port Arthur, the route intersects
TX 87. Turn south (right) and continue through town.
You'll cross the Gulf Intercoastal Waterway by bridge, and
in a few more miles you'll catch your first sight of the Gulf
of Mexico. For the next 65 miles, the road—which is
straight, usually empty, often gnawed along the seaward
edge by recent storms—takes you along the edge of the
beach past Sea Rim State Park, through McFaddin National
Wildlife Refuge, and eventually to Port Bolivar. Gas
stations along this road are few and seem to keep
unpredictable hours, so be sure you have a full tank
before you leave Port Arthur.

(For a more direct back-road route that saves about 30
miles of driving, bypasses the urban freeway hassles of
Beaumont and Port Arthur, and can bring you to
Galveston earlier—missing Sea Rim State Park, McFaddin

National Wildlife Refuge, and more than half of the northern Gulf Coast—simply turn south on TX 326 about 10 miles south of the road to the Big Thicket Visitors Center on US 69/287 at Kountze. Follow this road straight ahead. Although it changes designations several times—to Road 365, then to Road 1406, and finally, after crossing Interstate 10, to TX 124—it's all the same road. The whole 60-mile route brings you to the Gulf at High Island, from which it is a 27-mile drive along the beach to Port Bolivar.)

At Port Bolivar, the highway will lead you into the line for the ferry to Galveston. The free ferry trip takes about 15 minutes; boats run 24 hours a day. Warning: this ferry can be extremely crowded on weekends, making for a long wait.

When you disembark on Galveston Island, you will still be on TX 87 (here designated 2nd Street). Drive to the Gulf side of the island and either veer left onto Seawall Boulevard (the north end of the beachfront resort area, which becomes Road 3005 to Galveston Island State Park) or stay on TX 87 as it becomes Broadway Avenue, which takes you near the historic districts of town (watch for signs). Eventually, Broadway runs into Interstate 45 northbound to Houston, where you probably don't want to go just yet. To avoid leaving Galveston by accident, don't cross the large bridge.

Sightseeing Highlights
▲▲Alabama-Coushatta Indian Reservation—All of Texas's original Native American inhabitants are gone now. The Apaches were banished to New Mexico and the Comanches to Oklahoma. The Tejas, for whom the state was named, and the giant Karankawas were exterminated. There are only two small Indian reservations in Texas today. One belongs to the Alabama-Coushatta, two closely related groups of Creek people whose ancestors left Alabama in the mid-1700s to avoid getting involved in the conflict between the French and the English. After settling here in the Big Thicket, they found themselves caught up in a different conflict—between Texans and Mexicans. They agreed with Sam Houston to remain neutral in the

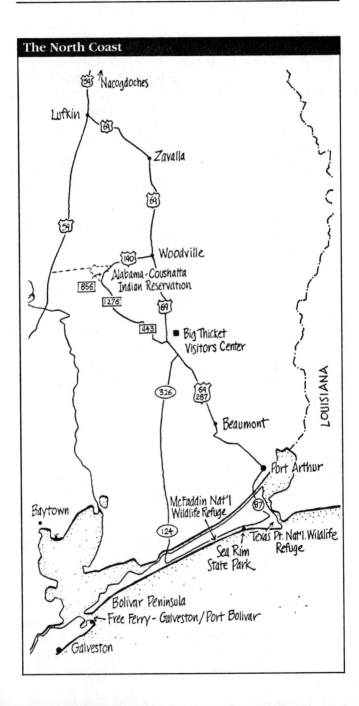

The North Coast

Texas War for Independence, and in return they received this 4,600-acre tract of land when the revolution succeeded.

Tourism is the tribe's livelihood. You can buy tickets for a train ride around the reservation, a Land Rover bus trip into the Big Thicket, an Indian dance performance, or a tour of a "living Indian village" re-creating ancestral ways. Tickets, which include all activities, cost $11 for adults and $9 for children ages 4 to 10. Tours are conducted during the spring and fall months on Friday and Saturday between the hours of 10:00 a.m. and 5:00 p.m., Sunday 12:30 to 5:00 p.m.; during the summer months Monday through Saturday 10:00 a.m. to 6:00 p.m., Sunday 12:30 to 6:00 p.m. Dance performances follow the same schedule but are held only on weekends in the spring and fall. There are no tours or dances during the winter months. Also at the Indian village, open on the same hours and days as the tours operate, are a small tribal museum, a restaurant, and a gift shop displaying tribal arts and crafts, notably beadwork and unusual baskets woven in the shapes of animals. A grocery store, laundromat, and RV campground operate year-round.

▲▲▲**Big Thicket National Preserve**—Two centuries ago, the dense forest known as the Big Thicket stretched from the Sabine River all the way to the site of modern-day Houston. It posed a formidable obstacle to settlement. Spanish colonists rarely ventured into it, and pioneers from the United States took long detours to avoid it. But after large-scale timber operations began in East Texas in the late 1870s, the ancient cypress and hardwoods were cut at a rate rivaling the destruction of tropical rain forests today. Worse yet, lumber companies poisoned the ground to prevent native vegetation from growing back and planted monocultural stands of fast-growing pines. Miraculously, a few hard-to-reach parts of the Big Thicket—about 8 percent of the original forest—survived.

To save these last fragments of primeval wilderness in Texas for future generations, in 1974 the federal government created Big Thicket National Preserve. Managed by the National Park Service, the 84,550-acre preserve consists of 12 separate units and four river corridors. The land here is remarkable in that so many different eco-systems—those of the southeastern swamps, Appalachian Mountains, eastern hardwood forests, central plains, and southwestern deserts—meet in a small area. Swampy subtropical cypress strands exist side-by-side with sandhills so arid that, despite 55 inches of annual rainfall, only cactus and yucca grow there. Nearby, sharp-eyed naturalists may recognize four of the five species of insect-eating plants that grow in the United States. In fact, the diversity of animal and plant life in the Big Thicket is so unique that in 1981 the preserve was designated a Man and Biosphere Reserve by UNESCO. The Sierra Club, U.S. Congressman Charles Wilson, and Senator Lloyd Bentsen are now trying to add another 14,000 acres to Big Thicket National Preserve.

The easiest way to see a quick sample of the Big Thicket is to hike the Kirby Nature Trail, which starts from the information station. This double loop trail—1-mile inner loop or 2-mile outer loop—takes you through varied pine and hardwood forest to a cypress slough on the Village Creek floodplain.

While most of the preserve is not penetrated by either road or hiking trail but can only be reached by canoe, the information center provides maps and information on several places where you can explore parts of the Big Thicket on foot. Adventuresome visitors with plenty of time may wish to get directions to the Turkey Creek Trail, at 9 miles one way, the longest trail in the park. Carnivorous plant enthusiasts should check out the 1-mile Sundew Trail and the ¼-mile Pitcher Plant trail. All three trailheads are challenging to search for along back roads within 20 miles of the information center; when you find one of them, you'll have a rare fragment of East Texas wilderness all to yourself.

The information center is open daily, closed Tuesday and Wednesday during the winter months. Ranger-guided nature walks are conducted on weekends. There are no camping facilities within the preserve, and pets are not allowed in the backcountry. Admission is free.

▲**Sea Rim State Park** and **McFaddin National Wildlife**

Refuge—The 5.2 miles of beach within the state park have freshwater wetlands on one side and the Gulf of Mexico on the other. The marshes here and in adjoining McFaddin National Wildlife Refuge harbor one of the densest alligator populations in Texas and, some naturalists claim, the state's last free-roaming, elusive red wolves, as well as numerous egrets, herons, and other large wading birds. Watch for them along the boardwalk nature trail, the state park's most interesting feature.

The park also has a full-hookup campground and plenty of camping space on the beach. It may sound tempting to stop here and let the gentle waves of the Gulf lull you to sleep tonight, but be warned: this part of the Texas coast is for those who love nature in spite of her blemishes. The wetlands breed clouds of mosquitoes, no-see-ums, and biting flies. You'll be sorry if you find yourself here after sundown without a good supply of mosquito coils. If you notice that everyone else is sunbathing and you're the only one swimming, it could be because of the sharks that cruise these waters from time to time. But don't let me discourage you. A beach is a beach. While the beaches will improve as you spend the next several days following the Gulf Coast south to the Texas tropics, this is the emptiest expanse of beach you can reach by car. The day-use fee at Sea Rim State Park is $2 per vehicle. Just south of the park, in McFaddin National Wildlife Refuge, are vehicle-accessible beach areas you can enjoy for free.

Lodging

At the end of today's trail is Galveston. For this itinerary, I suggest spending three nights in this historic beachfront city, which merits a day of exploration and also makes for a good home base while visiting Houston on a day trip. While room rates tend to run high in Galveston, especially during the summer months, similar accommodations cost more in Houston. It is worth noting, though, that room rates in Galveston are much higher on weekends, while many Houston hotels offer special discount rates on weekends. Since Galveston is practically on the front doorstep of Houston (about thirty times Galveston's size and without a beach of its own), it becomes very crowded on weekends, when hotel reservations are essential. During the week, you'll need reservations only if you're planning to stay at a B&B.

The Galveston lodging scene presents several attractive but quite different possibilities. You can stay in a resort hotel overlooking the beach, a Victorian-style grand hotel in the downtown Strand Historic District, or a bed and breakfast in the East End Historic District.

Among beachfront hotels, the **Hotel Galvez** is the only one included on the National Register of Historic Places. At 2024 Seawall Boulevard, (409) 765-7721, this 1911 resort was recently restored and is operated by Marriott Hotels. Rooms run $100 to $130 year-round.

Slightly lower rates on the beachfront can be found at **La Quinta Inn** (1402 Seawall Boulevard, 409-763-1224, $72 and up in the spring and summer months, $58 and up off-season) and the **Commodore on the Beach** (3618 Seawall Boulevard, 409-763-2375, $80 and up on spring and summer weekends, $64 and up on weekdays, and as low as $40 off-season).

Downtown in the Strand Historic District is the **Tremont House** (2300 Ship's Mechanic Row, 409-763-0300 or 800-874-2300 nationwide), a luxurious reconstruction by one of the leaders of Galveston's historic restoration movement. In a lavishly face-lifted Victorian commercial building, the interior re-creates the look of Galveston's original Tremont House (1839), which was considered the finest hotel in Texas in the nineteenth century but fell into disrepair after the hurricane of 1900 and was later torn down. Rooms for two range from $130 up.

Small, elegant bed and breakfasts in and around the East Side Historic District include the **Gilded Thistle** (1805 Broadway, 409-763-0194, $110-$135), the **Matali** (1727 Sealey on the corner of 18th Street, 409-763-4526, $75-$90), and the **Victorian Inn** (511 17th Street, 409-762-3235, $50-$135).

Budget accommodations are few and far between in Galveston. Your best bets are the **Day's Inn** (6107 Broadway, 740-2491, doubles from $55 on weekends and

$45 on weekdays May through Labor Day, from $30 off-
season), the **Motel 6** (7404 Broadway, 740-3794, doubles
from about $35), and other motels far from the beach
along the highway to Houston.

Galveston Camping
The best camping in the Galveston area is at **Galveston
Island State Park**, about 11 miles south of town on
County Road 3005. Campsites, nearly all with full
hookups, are on a broad lawn adjoining one of the most
attractive stretches of beach on the island. The camping
fee is $11 per night. As in all Texas state parks, the office
closes at 5:00 p.m. but the park entrance is not locked up
until 10:00 p.m., so if you arrive late, take any unoccupied
site, and a ranger will be around early to leave a note
reminding you to pay the camping fee by 9:00 a.m. Unless
you arrive by 5:00 p.m., however, you won't be given the
combination to open the park gate after 10:00 p.m., a
problem if you want to enjoy dinner and nightlife in
Galveston this evening. The solution? Talk Texas Friendly
with fellow campers, and they'll probably reveal the combination.

Food
At heart, Galveston is an overgrown fishing village.
Seafood, particularly shrimp, is the local specialty. The best
reputation on the beach belongs to **Gaido's**, 3818 Seawall
Boulevard, 762-9625, which has been operated by the
same family for over seventy years. It's generally believed
to be impossible to get through the door on weekend
evenings. (For lunch it's easier, and on weeknights there's
no problem.) Prices are moderate. Closed Mondays.

Another Galveston beachfront legend is the spicy,
almost absurdly affordable Cajun-style boiled shrimp
served at **Benno's on the Beach**, Seawall at 12th Street,
762-4621, open daily for lunch and dinner.

Away from the beach in the Strand district, follow 20th
Street to the wharf to locate **Hill's Pier 19** (763-7087). At
this rather expensive cafeteria (you pick your food, then
they cook it before your eyes), the real attraction is the

view. You can dine at sunset and watch the shrimp boats
unload, or stop in for lunch and watch big oceangoing
ships glide by.

But suppose you don't want seafood? Suppose you've
got an insatiable craving for real Texas meat, maybe
barbecued ribs or a big burger? **The Warehouse**, a block
off the Strand at 101 14th Street (765-9995), serves huge
portions at low prices with a beer ad ambience daily for
lunch and dinner.

While you're on the Strand, check out the gourmet picnic items and deli po'boys at the **Old Strand Emporium**,
2112 The Strand, 763-9445, open daily from 10:00 a.m. to
6:00 p.m. For dessert, drop by the Gay Nineties-style soda
fountain at **La King's Confectionary**, 2323 The Strand
(762-6100), open daily until 10:00 p.m.

GALVESTON

Galveston (pop. 60,000) is Houston's beach resort, but that's only half the story. After splashing in the surf and getting sand between your toes, you'll have all afternoon to explore the other half and learn about the town's proud history when it was Texas's capital, largest city, and main shipping port. The few nineteenth-century buildings that survived the killer hurricane of 1900 have been restored to create three historic districts in the central part of town, presenting you with the chance to explore several elegant old mansions and a century-old sailing ship.

Suggested Schedule

Morning	Relax at the beach.
1:00 p.m.	Visit one or more historic homes such as the Ashton Villa, the Bishop's Palace, or the 1839 Williams Home.
3:00 p.m.	Stop in at the Strand Visitors Center, then stroll the Strand.
4:00 p.m.	See the *Elissa.*
6:00 p.m.	Dinner.
Evening	Spend the night in Galveston or camp by the beach.

Galveston

For half its history, Galveston was the major seaport in Texas, beginning around 1817 under the name of Campeachy as a stronghold for pirate Jean Lafitte. In 1836 Galveston became the temporary capital of the Republic, and by the 1890s it was the largest city in Texas. But a hurricane in 1900 swept the island with tidal waves 20 feet deep and winds over 100 miles an hour, killing 6,000 people and leaving Galveston in rubble. Since then, virtually all commercial ships have docked instead on the inland side of Galveston Bay and up the ship channel at Houston, and Galveston has rebuilt itself to 2 percent of modern metropolitan Houston's size. Shrimp fishing, still a major industry, was the mainstay of Galveston's economy until the 1970s, when large-scale tourist development began. Today, in many places the Gulf side of the island is lined with resort hotels, condominium developments, and custom houses built on stilts or concrete pillars to let the inevitable next hurricane wash beneath their living room carpets. Away from the beach, big-budget historic restoration projects have been going on to provide visitors with something to see besides the endless beach. Few structures in Galveston survived the 1900 hurricane, and the oldest was built after the Texas War of Independence, so Galveston's antiquities are recent compared with those you'll see in San Antonio and El Paso. But in this part of the state, next door to Houston where everything is new, Galveston is old enough.

Seawall Boulevard is the beachfront drive and tourist zone. It intersects both the road from the ferry and Broadway (I-45 to Houston) near the north end of the island, then follows the Gulf Coast to become Farm Road 3005, the coastal road you'll want to take when leaving the area on Day 7. Most historic homes are on side streets marked by small signs from Broadway Avenue (TX 87, which becomes I-45 to Houston as it leaves the island). The Strand, the downtown historic district, is on the bay side of the island. To get there, turn north on 25th Street from either Seawall Boulevard or Broadway and keep going until you reach the waterfront.

Sightseeing Highlights

▲▲▲**Galveston Beaches**—Galveston Island has 32 miles of beach. While it may not be the widest or wildest stretch of beach on the Texas coast, it is certainly the cleanest, constantly patrolled by park department employees and volunteer groups ready to pounce on discarded plastic and other debris that tends to drift to shore here from as far away as south Florida.

All Texas beaches are public by state law. You can even pitch camp on the beach in front of a condominium if you want to—but you won't, because there are more secluded

Galveston

(Map shows: 34th St., 31st St., Rosenberg Ave., Strand District, The Elissa, Broadway, Ave. O, Ashton Villa, Bishop's Palace, Samuel May Williams Home, 145, Port Bolivar Ferry, Broadway, Seawall, Galveston Island State Park, GULF OF MEXICO)

spots a few miles farther down the coast. The in-town beaches on the eastern tip of the island at R. A. Apffel Park and along Seawall past the resort hotels are packed with bodies, beautiful and otherwise, slathered with suntan lotion and shimmering with salt water, on most summer days and nice weather weekends. You can be one of them.

Off-season weekdays find the city beaches so quiet that you might as well drive down to a more remote part of the island and enjoy the solitude. Several beachfront parks provide public access to the shore. Along Farm Road 3005 down the coast are Seven Mile Beach Park, Galveston County Beach Pocket Park 1 (near 7 Mile Road), Galveston County Beach Pocket Park 2 (near 9 Mile Road), and Galveston Island State Park (near 13 Mile Road). There is a parking charge at the two Beach Pocket parks, which are only open from mid-March through mid-October. Galveston Island State Park (see Day 4 Camping information) charges $2 per vehicle. During the peak season, mid-March through mid-September, motor vehicles are not allowed on the beaches except at designated parking areas. The rest of the year, the beach is open to cars and recreational vehicles.

▲▲**Historic Homes**—At Broadway and 14th on the edge of Galveston's East Side Historic District stands the Bishop's Palace, completed in 1893 at a cost of $250,000. The stone mansion served as a haven for hundreds of storm refugees after the hurricane of 1900. It was purchased by the Catholic church in 1923 and used as the Bishop of Galveston's residence until 1950. The Bishop's Palace is open to the public Monday through Saturday from 10:00 a.m. to 5:00 p.m. and Sunday from 12:00 noon to 5:00 p.m. during the summer months, daily except Tuesday from 12:00 noon to 4:00 p.m. the rest of the year. Admission is $3.50 per adult, $2 for students ages 13 to 18, and 50 cents for children under 12.

The 1839 Williams Home, in the East Side Historic District at 3601 Avenue P, is the oldest home on Galveston Island. It was built by Samuel May Williams, the man who financed the Texas War for Independence. An audiovisual presentation at the beginning of the self-guided tour tells the Williams family's story. The Williams home is open daily from 12:00 noon to 4:00 p.m. Admission is $3 per adult, $2.50 for senior citizens and students.

At Broadway and 24th, the gingerbready Ashton Villa offers tours and a multimedia show about the hurricane of 1900, which this three-story Italianate mansion survived. It is open daily from 10:00 a.m. to 3:00 p.m. during the summer months, daily from 11:00 a.m. to 3:00 p.m. the rest of the year. Admission is $4 for adults, $3.50 for senior citizens and students.

▲▲**The Strand**—Once known as the "Wall Street of the Southwest," The Strand was the most important commercial district in Texas and one of the leading cotton markets in the world during the late nineteenth century. Rather than raze the old iron-fronted buildings for urban renewal, the city of Galveston and the Galveston Historical Foundation chose to undertake an ambitious, ongoing restoration of six blocks along The Strand, and the "bring back the past" fervor has spread throughout the downtown area. Start your stroll at the Strand Visitors Center, 2016 Strand, where you can rent a cassette deck and tape for a self-guided audio tour or pick up a free walking tour brochure.

A unique place to browse and perhaps buy an odd piece of camping equipment is the claustrophobic Colonel Bubbie's Strand Surplus Senter at The Strand and 22nd Street, headquarters of one of the world's largest military surplus enterprises. Some items date back to the Spanish-American War and even the Civil War. The store is open Monday through Saturday from 10:00 a.m. to 4:00 p.m.

The showpiece of the Strand district is the sailing ship *Elissa*, one of the oldest merchant vessels afloat. Built in Scotland in 1877, the ship docked at Galveston often during the late nineteenth century and sailed the world's oceans for nearly a century before being seized in Greece with a cargo of smuggled cigarettes in 1970. The Galveston Historical Foundation had the ship towed here in 1975, and enthusiastic volunteer workers along with $3.6 million in contributions restored it to full glory. A free film at the Strand Visitors Center tells the story of the restoration. The *Elissa* is permanently docked at Pier 21 on the waterfront, at Water and 22nd Street one block north of The Strand. The ship contains maritime historical exhibits. There is also a gift shop, and a replica of part of the ship's deck and rigging has been built on the dock to give children a safe place to scramble. The *Elissa* is open daily from 10:00 a.m. to 5:00 p.m., later during the summer months. Admission is $5 for adults, $4 for senior citizens, military personnel, and students ages 7 to 18, maximum $16 per family.

The *Colonel*, a three-deck paddlewheel tour boat, departs from the wharf near the *Elissa* for two-hour sightseeing cruises of Galveston Bay at 12:00 noon, 2:00 and 4:00 p.m. daily. The cost is $6 per person. There are also adults-only dinner and moonlight cruises, $27.50 per person. For current schedule and reservations, call 763-4666.

HOUSTON

Texas's major port city, where oil importing and refining
are the principal industries, is not a major tourist destination. Freeway traffic and sheer size overwhelm many
visitors, but a day trip into the city can prove rewarding as
you explore the nerve center of America's space program,
then "cruise the Loop" and discover sights that include a
fabulously decorated mansion-turned-museum, an ultraelegant shopping mall, and the original domed sports
stadium. This evening, on your way back to Galveston,
visit the birthplace of Texas independence and a truly vast
"urban cowboy" honky-tonk.

Suggested Schedule

8:00 a.m.	Leave Galveston.
9:00 a.m.	Visit the Lyndon B. Johnson Space Center.
11:30 a.m.	Lunch in the space center cafeteria.
12:00 noon	Drive to Houston.
1:00 p.m.	Drive through Memorial Park and visit Bayou Bend.
3:00 p.m.	Go shopping at the Galleria or tour the Astrodome.
4:00 p.m.	Get out of Houston ahead of rush-hour traffic.
5:00 p.m.	Visit San Jacinto State Historical Park
Evening	Two-step, battle the mechanical bull, or just watch the festivities at Gilley's.
Late	Return to Galveston for the night.

Travel Route: Galveston to Houston
(70 miles each way)

From Galveston, drive north on Interstate 45 for 25 miles
to the NASA Road exit. The Lyndon B. Johnson Space
Center is 3 miles east of the interstate; just follow the
big signs.

From the space center, get back on I-45 and continue north. After 15 miles, the interstate meets I-610, the Loop Freeway around central Houston. Take I-610 northbound (the East Loop). Follow I-610 counterclockwise all the way around the city; the Houston sightseeing highlights I suggest below are all near the Loop. When you complete the circuit and come back to I-45 southbound to Galveston, get on it and drive back to Galveston.

(If you wish to visit San Jacinto Battlefield, stay on the Loop for 2 more miles after passing I-45 and take exit 30 onto TX 225—the La Porte Freeway. After driving about 20 miles, turn north on TX 134—Battleground Road—and continue for 3 miles to the park. On leaving, head back the way you came on TX 225 to Pasadena and take Spur 8, the East Sam Houston Freeway, south to rejoin I-45 south to Galveston. The East Sam Houston Freeway intersects Spencer Highway, the street where you'll find Gilley's.)

Houston

The largest city in Texas and fourth largest in the United States, Houston (pop. 3,750,000) can seem overwhelming and not the kind of place you would choose to spend much of your vacation. Tourism does not play a major role in the city's economy, and it's easy to waste a good part of a one-day visit lost on, or looking for, the freeways.

Yet Houston has its own distinctive character and is not shy about showing it. One key to understanding the city is that it has no zoning laws. Instead of urban planning, Houston has grown randomly according to the whims of real estate developers, as you can see when driving around the Loop. It's hard to identify the downtown area from the skyline because skyscrapers rise from a dozen different islands around the city. Skyscrapers are everywhere you look. At this writing, Houston has more skyscrapers under construction than any other city in the nation. The Transco Building near the Galleria is the tallest building in the world outside of a downtown area.

The city was named after Sam Houston, the revolutionary leader and hero of the Battle of San Jacinto who became the first president of the Republic of Texas. It's probably a good thing, too. If they had decided to name a different town after Sam, this one might have wound up being named after its leading citizens and benefactors, the Hogg family (more about them below).

The secret to finding your way around Houston is that practically every place you want to go is accessible from the Loop Freeway, I-610, which goes all the way around the city. The Houston sightseeing highlights listed below, designed to give you a sampling of the city in a single day and get you out of town before rush hour, are in sequence around the Loop, traveling counterclockwise, starting and ending at the Gulf Freeway (I-45). To make navigation simpler, the four sides of the Loop are designated according to which side of downtown they're on. You'll proceed north on the East Loop, west on the North Loop, south on the West Loop, and back to I-45 on the South Loop.

Sightseeing Highlights
▲▲▲**Space Center Houston**—The Lyndon B. Johnson Space Center is Mission Control, the command post for all NASA manned space flights from the first Mercury capsules in the 1960s to today's space shuttle projects. Park at the visitor parking lot near the rocket park and walk down Avenue D to the visitor center, called Space Center Houston, where you'll see collected space program artifacts such as a lunar landing craft, space suits, and moon rocks. There is also an Omnimax theater showing *To Be an Astronaut.*

A self-guided tour takes you to Building 30, the Mission Control Center itself, full of computer terminals. The guided tour of Mission Control lasts about 35 minutes. After leaving the Mission Control Center, you go to Building 5, the Mission Simulation and Training Facility. There you'll see the elaborate flight simulators where astronauts train for space shuttle missions.

To complete the tour of the space center, board a tram to the Space Shuttle Orbiter Training Facility, where you can see full-scale Space Shuttle trainers. Nearby, Building 31A houses what may be the strangest curiosity in the

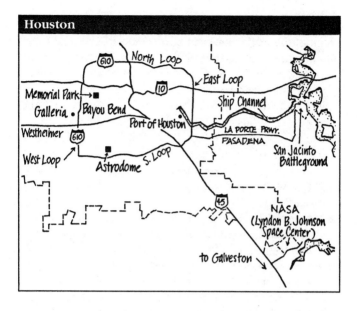

Houston

space center complex. Astronauts brought back over 800 pounds of moon rocks from various lunar missions. Scientists around the world are studying some of them, while others are in museums, but most of the moon rocks are stored in this Lunar Sample Building. You may never again have a chance to see as many extraterrestrial rocks in one place. You'll have a chance to see how space geologists test them, too.

Space Center Houston is open daily from 9:00 a.m. to 7:00 p.m. Admission is $8.75 for adults, and $5.25 for children ages 4 to 12.

▲**Port of Houston**—Houston is the United States' leading port for international shipping and the third-largest port in terms of total tonnage. This may seem odd, since the sea-coast is 50 miles away. To establish a Texas seaport far enough inland to be safe from hurricanes, the federal government in 1908 dredged a ship canal up Buffalo Bayou. You can watch the Houston Turning Basin, designed to let ships reverse direction at the end of the narrow channel, from the observation deck atop Gate 9 (go through Gate 8) on Clinton Road. More than 4,000 ships dock here each year.

The best way to see the harbor and wharves is from the deck of the inspection boat *Sam Houston*. The boat runs 90-minute tours year-round on Monday, Tuesday, Wednesday, Friday, and Saturday at 10:00 a.m. and 2:30 p.m., Thursday and Sunday 2:30 p.m. only; no tours in July. The boat tour is free, but there's a catch: you need to make reservations as much as two months in advance. Write Port of Houston, P.O. Box 2562, Houston, TX 77252, or call (713) 670-2416.

To reach the Port of Houston, take exit 28 from the Loop and follow the signs on Wayside Drive and Avenue R to Clinton Road.

▲**Memorial Park**—Exit the West Loop at Memorial Drive and proceed east through Memorial Park. The park was donated to the city in the 1920s by Will Hogg, the Houston real estate tycoon who developed the River Oaks neighborhood of mansions across Buffalo Bayou from the park. Hogg's stipulation was that if the land were ever used as anything other than a park, the city would forfeit it. Today the park is a popular urban playground with a public golf course, tennis courts, polo grounds, baseball diamonds, an archery range, and a 3-mile jogging course.

The Houston Arboretum and Nature Center, off Woodway Drive in the southwest corner of the park, preserves 260 acres of natural plant and animal habitat along the bank of Buffalo Bayou. Five miles of walking trails let you take a peaceful stroll in the woods to the distant rumble of traffic on the Loop. The arboretum's exhibit room is open daily from 9:00 a.m. to 5:00 p.m. The grounds are open daily from 8:30 a.m. until 6:00 p.m. Admission is free.

▲**Bayou Bend**—James Stephen Hogg, who was the state's first native-born governor in the 1890s, named his daughter Ima. Rising above the name, she became Houston's leading patron of the arts. As her crowning achievement, Ima Hogg left her 28-room antebellum mansion and its furnishings to the Houston Museum of Fine Arts. (The main unit of the museum, along with the museum of natural history, the planetarium, and the zoo, is in Hermann Park, off the Southwest Freeway—US 59—between downtown and the Astrodome, near Rice University.) Bayou Bend, on a beautifully landscaped 14-acre estate overlooking Buffalo Bayou, contains one of the finest collections in existence of seventeenth- to nineteenth-century American decorative items and furnishings. Bayou Bend is across the bayou from the east side of Memorial Park. From Memorial Drive, take Westcott Street south for one-half mile. The gardens and landscaped grounds remain open to the public ($3 adult admission) Tuesday to Saturday 10:00 a.m. to 5:00 p.m. The mansion is open for tours Tuesday through Friday from 9:00 a.m. to 4:00 p.m. and Saturday from 10:00 a.m. to 12:45 p.m., closed Sundays. Tours cost $7.50 to $10, depending on length; children under 10 free. For guided tour information and reservations, write Tour Secretary, Bayou Bend, Box 130157, Houston, TX 77219, or call (713) 529-8773.

▲**The Galleria**—This is Houston's most elegant shopping mall, where stores include Neiman Marcus, Tiffany's, Lord & Taylor, and the like. Dallas has a similar Galleria mall, but in Houston the Galleria has become the hub of a "mini-downtown" (variously known as The Strip, The Miracle Mile, or the Magic Circle) with its own skyscrapers, major hotels, and many exclusive places to shop. Parking is free at the Galleria, but low overhead clearance puts the parking lot off limits to tall RVs. From the West Loop, take the Westheimer Road exit westbound and you're there.

▲**The Astrodome**—When it was built in 1965, the Astrodome was the first domed indoor sports stadium. Taller than a 20-story building, the dome encloses an area of about 330,000 square feet lit by 5,000 skylights. The Houston Oilers (football), Gamblers (football), and Astros (baseball), as well as the University of Houston Cougars (football), play their home games here. The Astrodome also hosts other events ranging from livestock shows and rodeos to motorcycle races. One-hour tours of the stadium, including a video presentation, a look at the highest box seats and the press box plus a demonstration of the high-tech scoreboard, are offered daily at 11:00 a.m., 1:00 and 3:00 p.m., and in July and August 5:00 p.m. except when an evening event is scheduled. The tour costs $4 per adult and $3 for children ages 4 to 11 and senior citizens. For current tour and event information, call 799-9544. To get there, take the Astrodome exit from the South Loop.

Across the freeway is Astroworld, Houston's largest amusement park, containing nine theme areas and 100 rides. It is open daily from 11:00 a.m. to 10:00 p.m. Memorial Day to Labor Day, weekends only from 10:00 a.m. to 10:00 p.m. in the spring and fall months, closed in winter. Admission is $23.95 for adults, $15.95 for children under 54 inches tall, free for children under 3.

▲**San Jacinto Battleground State Historical Park—** Although it is less famous than the Alamo, this is the spot where Texas won its independence from Mexico. After disastrous defeats at the Alamo (see Day 11) and Goliad (120 miles east of San Antonio, not on this itinerary), the ragtag army of Texas patriots under Sam Houston's command was pursued by the much larger Mexican army of General Santa Anna, who was bent on driving them into the sea. Here, a short drive from the city that bears his name, Houston's guerrillas turned on the Mexicans, attacking their camp during afternoon fiesta on April 21, 1836, the most important date in Texas history books. Houston captured General Santa Anna, and the ransom price was freedom for Texas. Today, the spot is marked by a 570-foot tower, the world's largest masonry monument, affording a panoramic view of the most populous part of the Texas coast. In the base of the tower is the San Jacinto Museum of History, containing artifacts from early Indian civilizations, the War for Independence, and the Civil War. The park is open daily, 9:00 a.m. to 6:00 p.m. Museum admission is free; the elevator to the top of the tower costs $2 for adults, 50 cents for children under 12. A slide show recalling the Battle of San Jacinto costs $3.50 per adult and $2 per child under 12. Also at San Jacinto Battleground is the Battleship *Texas*, which served in both world wars. It can be toured between 10:00 a.m. and 5:00 p.m. The cost is $2 per adult, $1.50 for children 6 to 12.

Lodging
Hotels in Houston tend to be big, costly, and business-oriented. That's why I suggest making your visit to

Houston a day trip and spending another night at your lodging or campsite in the Galveston area. On weekends, however, the situation is different. Galveston's resort hotels can fill up quickly on Fridays and Saturdays, and their room rates skyrocket on weekends. In Houston, though, the big hotels' busiest times are weekdays, and many offer special bargain rates on Friday, Saturday, and Sunday nights. For example, the **Houstonian Hotel** (111 North Post Oak Lane, across the West Loop from Memorial Park, 800-392-0784 in Texas or 800-231-2759 nationwide) costs $139 to $149 a night during the week but only $89 on weekends. The **Westin Galleria** (5060 W. Alabama; 713-960-8100) off Westheimer two blocks from the Galleria Mall costs $140 on weekdays but $90 on weekends. **Holiday Inn Crowne Plaza** (2222 West Loop South, 713-961-7272 or 800-327-6213) costs $114 to $159 on weekdays and $69 to $104 on weekends. The **Marriott Westloop by the Galleria** (1750 West Loop South; 713-960-0111) is $109 to $149 on weekdays and $89 on weekends.

Food

Exceptional restaurants in all price ranges abound in the Galleria vicinity. In the mall itself, the restaurant at Marshall Field's is one of the finest department store restaurants you'll find anywhere, serving soup, salad, and sandwiches as well as full dinners and luscious desserts during mall hours (lunch and dinner only, closed Sundays). **Vie de France Café and Bakery**, 827-1007, on the second level of Galleria II, is an inexpensive café specializing in stuffed croissants. It serves breakfast, lunch, and dinner daily except Sundays. Nearby at 1842 Fountain View, the **Fountain View Cafe** serves up big breakfasts, burgers, and beautiful baked goods daily (open on weekends for breakfast and lunch only).

For an elegant dinner in the Galleria area, try **The Brownstone**, off Westheimer at 2736 Virginia, 520-5666. The menu features an eclectic assortment of nouveau fare billed as "continental cuisine with a New Orleans Italian flair," and the decor is rich with artwork and antiques. Tables are also available poolside on the casual patio.

Nightlife

The nightclub to visit on a first trip to the Houston area is **Gilley's**, located in the eastern suburb of Pasadena at 4500 Spencer Highway. (See the Travel Route above—Pasadena is on the way to San Jacinto Battlefield National Monument.) This huge honky-tonk with its mechanical bull, rodeo arena, and acres of dance floor came to national prominence in the 1970s as the location for the film *Urban Cowboy*, and today it's one of Houston's most popular tourist attractions. The club's owner, country-western singer Mickey Gilley, often performs there. At other times, Gilley's features various top country bands. It is open nightly. The cover charge for live entertainment varies. ror current performance information, call 941-7900.

DOWN THE GULF COAST

Driving halfway down the Texas coast, you'll discover what distinguishes this from any other seashore in America. It is mostly empty and sometimes completely inaccessible. The reason is the threat of occasional devastating hurricanes, rare enough that they're not likely to put a crimp in your vacation plans but common enough so that resort developers are reluctant to run the risk. Barrier island beaches span practically the whole length of the coast, and most of them are empty. Most of the coastline still belongs to wildlife, not to man. After detouring away from the Gulf of Mexico around the roadless Matagorda Peninsula, you can visit the wintering grounds of the whooping crane. Then you'll explore the "Texas Riviera," wintering grounds of a growing number of human snowbirds, which bears little resemblance to its European namesake. At the end of

Suggested Schedule

8:00 a.m.	Leaving the Galveston area, drive south along the barrier islands to the Brazosport Area.
9:00 a.m.	Detouring inland, drive to Port Lavaca.
11:30 p.m.	Take a side trip to the former site of Indianola to picnic and ponder the power of Mother Nature.
1:00 p.m.	Drive on to Austwell.
2:00 p.m.	Take the loop drive through Aransas National Wildlife Refuge. In winter, look for whooping cranes.
3:30 p.m.	Drive on to Rockport and Aransas Pass.
4:30 p.m.	Take the ferry over to Port Aransas on the northern tip of Mustang Island.
5:00 p.m.	Drive to Padre Island.
Evening	Camp on the beach at Padre Island National Seashore or spend the night on North Padre Island. (Noncampers may wish to stay in Rockport and visit Padre Island tomorrow.)

this leg of your journey is Padre Island National Seashore, one of the longest stretches of undeveloped beach in the United States. Here, you'll be at the same latitude as Tampa, Florida, on the far side of the Gulf.

Travel Route: Galveston to Corpus Christi (259 miles)
From Galveston, follow FR 3005 south along the beaches of Galveston Island and Follets Island (linked by a toll bridge) for 51 miles to Surfside Beach. This is one of nine small, independent, nearly adjoining towns collectively known as the Brazosport Area (pop. 53,000), although none of the towns is named Brazosport. Practically the only part of the Texas coast that is not an island, the Brazosport Area was an early seaport. Stephen F. Austin and the first 300 Anglo colonists in Texas landed there in 1821, making it the Texas counterpart of Plymouth Rock. Today the Brazosport Area has relatively little resort development, despite fine beaches, because of noxious petrochemical plants nearby.

In Surfside Beach, turn west (right) on TX 332 and follow the route signs for 20 miles through Clute and Lake Jackson to Brazoria, where you turn north (right) to follow TX 36 for 8 miles to West Columbia. There, proceed south (left) on TX 35 for 52 miles to Palacios, another 31 miles to Port Lavaca, and 20 more miles to where TX 316 exits east (left) to Austwell. If you wish to visit Aransas National Wildlife Refuge, exit here and follow the signs for a 20-mile detour to the refuge. Returning from the refuge, in Austwell take Farm Road 774, which zigzags south and west to bring you back to TX 35 several miles farther south than where you left. Whether you visit the refuge or not, continue south on TX 35 to Rockport and, 11 miles farther along, Aransas Pass.

The reason this travel route does not follow the shore line between the Brazosport Area and Rockport is that there is no road along the coast. In fact, Matagorda Island, the barrier island to the east of Port Lavaca and Aransas National Wildlife Refuge, is the most inaccessible section of the Texas Gulf Coast. No road goes there, and its nearly pristine wetlands and beaches are under the protection of

the state and the Nature Conservancy as a critical habitat
for wading birds and breeding ground for several
endangered species of sea turtles. Matagorda Island State
Park on the northern end of the island can only be reached
by boat.

From Aransas Pass, follow TX 361 east to the ferry dock,
where a free ferry carries vehicles 24 hours a day to Port
Aransas on the northern tip of Mustang Island. Keep an
eye out for dolphins near the ferry. On the island, follow
TX 361 south along the coast for about 18 miles to four-
lane Park Road 22. Continue along the coast for 9 miles to
Padre Island or turn inland to Corpus Christi.

Sightseeing Highlights
▲**Indianola**—At Port Lavaca, turn off to the east on TX
316 and drive 14 miles to Indianola. This ghost town
explains vividly why so much of the Texas coast is
undeveloped. In the mid-nineteenth century, Indianola was
one of the largest port cities in Texas, rivaling Galveston.
In 1875, a hurricane sent a tidal wave across the peninsula,
destroying the city and taking 900 lives. The survivors
rebuilt Indianola, but just 11 years later an even larger
hurricane wiped it off the face of the earth so completely
that only the ruined foundations you see here today
remained. For over a century, all but a few hardy fishermen have been content to leave the site of Indianola to the
sea and sand. Except for a state historical marker, there's
nothing much to see. It's an eloquent nothingness.
▲▲**Aransas National Wildlife Refuge**—Whooping
cranes are the star attraction of this 55,000-acre refuge, one
of the largest in Texas. In the 1940s, the cranes' number
had dwindled to 21, and their impending extinction made
many Americans aware of endangered species for the first
time. Today, while their numbers have increased to nearly
100, the cranes remain among the world's rarest birds.
They spend the summer at Wood Buffalo National Park in
Alberta, Canada, and each year scientists use radio tracking
devices to follow each crane on its southward migration to
its wintering ground at Texas Point, Matagorda Island, or
Aransas National Wildlife Refuge. Between December and

Galveston to Padre Island

GALVESTON

West Columbia ⑥⓪

③⑤

⑤⑥

Brazosport Area

③①⑥ Indianola

Aransas Nat'l Wildlife Refuge

③⑤

Rockport
Aransas Pass
Ferry Port Aransas

• GULF OF MEXICO •

CORPUS CHRISTI
to Padre Island

March, especially in the morning or late afternoon, if you
search the shoreline with one of the telescopes on the
viewing tower a short distance off the loop road through
the refuge, you're likely to see one of these majestic,
6-foot-tall white cranes. The park is also home to deer,
javelinas, armadillos, wild turkeys, and coyotes, all hard to
spot in the dense live oak scrub, as well as large birds
including the caracara, an eaglelike raptor more commonly
encountered in South America. Visit the alligator that lives
near the start of the loop road. 'Gators are common
enough in coastal Texas, but they're elusive; this will
probably be your best chance to see a really big one.
Aransas National Wildlife Refuge is open daily from sunrise
to sunset. Admission is $2 per vehicle. There is no over-
night camping.

▲**Rockport**—As soon as you cross the Copano Bay
Causeway on TX 35, you'll enter Fulton and hardly notice
as you cross into the larger, adjoining village of Rockport
(pop. 5,000). Recently, the two towns have been attracting
resident artists as well as winter snowbirds, so you'll find

plenty of art galleries and RV parks. To discover why these people find the community so appealing, take some extra time to explore the diversity of its little-known attractions. Goose Island State Park, 12 miles north of town, a popular fishing and bird-watching spot, also has a swimming beach and the largest live oak tree in Texas, estimated to be 2,000 years old ($2 per vehicle admission). Another favorite place to fish is Copano Bay Causeway State Park, a former causeway paralleling modern day TX 35 across the bay between the Goose Island turnoff and Fulton; you can walk out onto the fishing piers from either end for a small fee, though you cannot walk all the way across the bay because the central span is gone. The showpiece historic mansion in the area is the Fulton Mansion State Historic Structure (c. 1876) on Fulton Beach Road, a gingerbready 4-story, 30-room home built by a cattle baron, open Wednesday through Sunday 9:00 a.m. to 11:30 p.m. and 1:00 to 3:30 p.m., admission $3 for adults and $1.50 for children ages 6 to 12. Local artwork is on display at the Rockport Art Center, in a restored 1890s home on the harbor just off TX 35; admission is free. You'll also find several retail art galleries around town. Rockport has a mile-long swimming beach adjacent to the Connie Hagar Wildlife Preserve.

▲▲▲**Padre Island National Seashore**—This all-natural beach might as well be endless. It runs for 60 miles south from the entrance gate, which is the only access by road. The paved park road ends after 5 miles, and beyond that you can drive on the beach for another 5 miles. The other 50 miles are only passable by four-wheel drive or all-terrain vehicles—or on foot. (Bring as much water as you would for a day in the desert; there is no fresh water past the visitors center.) Even in a Jeep, the beach drive is a dead-end. You can only drive back the same way you came, so make sure you have a full tank of gas before you start. The lagoon side of the island is only accessible by boat. The mile-wide dunes between the two shores are off-limits to hikers except for the self-guided Grasslands Nature Trail near the entrance gate. The vegetation that anchors the sand dunes—salt-resistant plants such as sea

oats, beach tea, sea rockets, evening primrose, and morning glories—is so fragile that footsteps could destroy it;
wherever that happens, pieces of the island are washed
away by storms. The dunes are also home to rattlesnakes.

You have your choice of beach scenes here, from lively
to lonely. North Beach, the easiest to reach and the only
part where motor vehicles are not allowed, can be packed
with swimmers and sunbathers during the summer and on
warm weekends the rest of the year. Drive down South
Beach to Milepost 5 and walk south from there to find
expanses of sand that are lightly traveled any time and, on
off-season weekdays, often completely trackless.

The sea along Padre Island's beaches is shallow, and in
fair weather the surf is gentle and soothing. Swimmers will
find the water chilly during the winter months but comfortable the rest of the year. There are no lifeguards, so
children should be supervised closely, but the water is safe
for swimming all along the national seashore. The only
serious hazard is the Portuguese man-of-war, a jellyfish
that sometimes appears in hordes along the coast. If you
see some of these creatures, which look like pink-tinged
blue balloons, washed up on shore, then watch out for
them if you go in the water. Their slender, dangling
tentacles pack a painful sting. (The most effective painkiller
is urine. Sure, it sounds disgusting, but in case of emer-
gency, you'll be glad I told you.)

To bird-watchers, Padre Island is endlessly fascinating.
Three hundred fifty bird species make their homes here,
and you're sure to see laughing gulls, fairy terns, and
sandpipers galore, along with larger birds such as pelicans,
herons, egrets, and sandhill cranes.

For many, beachcombing is the most intriguing activity
on Padre Island. Seashells here are many and varied. The
largest are sea pens, so brittle that they're hard to take
home intact. Also common are giant cockles, bay scallops,
venus clams, sand dollars, and fragments of coral. A field
guide to seashells can help you identify other finds with
evocative names like Scotch bonnie, buttercup, sundial,
angel wing, turkey wing, and baby's ear. Shells tend to
wash up in some spots more than others, so you may walk

for a mile without seeing a single one, then suddenly come across enough beach treasures to fill up a lawn and leaf bag. If you leave Padre Island without a collection of free souvenirs, it's your own fault. Early morning is the best time for beachcombing, and for many that fact alone is reason enough to camp overnight here.

Admission to Padre Island National Wildlife Refuge is $4 per vehicle or, for pedestrians and cyclists, $1 per person.

Lodging

Corpus Christi's local bed and breakfast reservation service, **Sand Dollar Hospitality** (3605 Mendenhall, Corpus Christi, TX 78415, 512-853-1222), can arrange a homestay for you in one of more than a dozen private residences in Corpus Christi and Rockport. Rates range from under $40 to about $75 per night.

You'll find many condominium and apartment hotel complexes on North Padre Island near where TX 281 from Mustang Island intersects Park Road 22 to the national seashore. Most of them offer units for rent, and location, size, and cooking facilities make them an attractive option, especially for families traveling together. Call in advance to check availability at **Sea Horse Resort Condominiums** (14921 Windward Drive, 512-949-7041), **Surfside Condominium Apartments** (15005 Windward Drive, 512-949-8128), or **Anchor Resort Condominiums** (14802 Padre Island Drive, 512-949-8141). Condos on North Padre Island can also be booked through rental agencies such as **Padre Island Rental Clearinghouse** (14602 S. Padre Island Drive, 512-949-7003, or toll-free 800-242-0117 from Texas or 800-531-1030 nationwide). Condominium accommodations are pricey—typically around $150 a night during the summer months—but drop to around $75 a night during the off-season.

If the condo scene sounds less appealing than a simple motel room in a small coastal community that hasn't yet been taken over by big development, I suggest that you stop early on today's route in Rockport, where ma-and-pa motels are still the rule. Check out the **Village Inn** (503 N. Austin Street at TX 35, 512-729-6370) or the **Surfside**

Motel (1809 Broadway, 512-729-2348) and its neighbor, the **Sun Tan Motel** (1805 Broadway, 512-729-2179). Room rates in the Rockport area start below $40 a night. If you choose to stay in Rockport, allow an extra day in your itinerary to enjoy Padre Island National Seashore tomorrow.

Camping

Padre Island National Seashore presents an array of camping possibilities. The main developed campground, on your left from the paved road about 4 miles in from the entrance gate, is a large, paved parking lot with concrete picnic tables, water and electric hookups, and a $5 camping fee. This campground is not suitable for tenting, but it is perfectly located near the south end of North Beach. From the campground, you can take a short walk south to the most popular swimming beach or a long walk north along a part of the beach where vehicles are prohibited and seashells are abundant.

There is also a campground at Bird Island Basin, on the lagoon side of the island. To reach it, take the long paved side road on your right about 2 miles in from the entrance gate. This campground is popular with fishermen and bird-watchers but not with visitors who have an aversion to mosquito-infested swamps. Since it has the only boat ramp on Padre Island, it can be very crowded on weekends. There are no hookups; chemical restrooms are provided.

You can camp free anywhere on South Beach. Simply follow the main paved road all the way to the end and continue onto the beach, which you can drive in a motor home or passenger vehicle for a little more than 5 miles. All along this beach, camping is allowed between the beach "road" and the dunes. There is no drinking water or electricity, so you'll need to bring your own. Campfires are permitted on the beach.

Food

If you plan to camp on Padre Island National Seashore tonight, stop en route at Rockport or Aransas Pass to pick up plenty of picnic food, since there is no grocery store at the national seashore. With adequate provisions, you'll have the option of spending an extra day at the beach—a temptation that may prove irresistible if the weather cooperates tomorrow.

Corpus Christi has hundreds of restaurants, from fast food to family-style to fancy, but in researching this book I've been unable to discover many that seem special enough to recommend. As is true all along the Gulf Coast, you're never far from a seafood dinner. One place on North Padre Island that is worth searching for is **Snoopy's Pier** (10875 S. Padre Island Drive, 949-8815). This picnic-table rustic grill, popular with local fishermen long before tourism took over the island, serves freshly caught shrimp and other seafood lunches and dinners at prices that are hard to beat. But it's a little hard to find, on an unpaved road under the island end of the causeway to Corpus Christi. To locate it from Padre Island I had to drive over the causeway to the mainland, turn around and drive back across, then exit to the right immediately upon reaching the island. It was well worth the trip.

If you're spending the night in Rockport, the place to dine is the **Big Fisherman Restaurant**, 6 miles south on TX 35 and then west on Farm Road 1069, 729-1997. The food is fairly typical—seafood and steaks. It's the "decor" that makes this restaurant memorable; it's a virtual zoo of live local and tropical birds, with some wild animals as well.

THE TEXAS TROPICS

No need for an early start this morning. Take a long beach stroll on Padre Island National Seashore. Today's drive veers away from the coast to cross the vast King Ranch and brings you back to the seashore nearly 200 miles down the road—at the other end of Padre Island.

Suggested Schedule	
10:00 a.m.	Leave Padre Island. Drive through Corpus Christi and south to Kingsville.
11:30 a.m.	Take the self-guided auto tour at King Ranch.
12:15 p.m.	Lunch in Kingsville.
1:00 p.m.	Drive south across the King Ranch.
3:00 p.m.	In Harlingen, visit the Rio Grande Valley Museum or drive out to Laguna Atascosa Wildlife Refuge.
4:15 p.m.	Drive to Port Isabel and South Padre Island.
5:00 p.m.	Check into your campground or lodging.

Travel Route: Corpus Christi to South Padre Island (198 miles)

Return via Padre Island Drive (TX 358) through downtown Corpus Christi to where the freeway merges with I-37. Drive west on I-37 for 10 miles to exit 14, US 77. Head south on US 77 for 36 miles to Kingsville. In Kingsville, watch for the signs for TX 141 and turn west. The King Ranch headquarters and self-guided auto tour exits are to the west just past the outskirts of town.

After visiting the ranch, retrace your route back into town on TX 141 and return to US 77 southbound. Before venturing beyond Kingsville, make sure your gas tank is full. Past there are miles and miles of nothing but miles and miles. Continue on US 77 for 85 miles to Harlingen, then 11 more miles to the TX 100 exit. Take TX 100 east for 26 miles to Port Isabel. The Queen Isabella Causeway, the longest bridge in Texas, crosses the lagoon to South Padre Island.

Sightseeing Highlights
▲▲King Ranch—The largest ranch in Texas (823,000 contiguous acres) was founded in 1853 by Richard King, a former Rio Grande riverboat captain. He relocated an entire Mexican village onto the ranch to provide a steady labor supply. Like everybody else in Texas at the time, Captain King raised longhorns at first, but then he developed the Santa Gertrudis breed, part Brahma and part shorthorn, hardy enough to survive here in the Wild Horse Desert, yet producing tenderer beef that brought a better price up north. It was the first new cattle breed to be developed in the Western Hemisphere. Today, the King Ranch is still owned by Captain King's heirs. Additional ranchlands in other states and six foreign countries make it the largest privately owned ranch in the world. Take the 12-mile self-guided tour from the ranch headquarters, west off TX 141, to see various aspects of the ranching operation such as feedlots and an auction ring. A cassette tape tour that explains it all can be rented for $3. The ranch drive is open from 9:00 a.m. to 4:00 p.m., free.
▲Rio Grande Valley Museum—This museum at Boxwood and Rainbow streets in Harlingen has a large map of the Lower Rio Grande Valley on which you push buttons to light up destinations and gain a vivid orientation. The museum also contains rock and shell collections, as well as historical artifacts from all over the valley. Besides the main museum, the complex includes Harlingen's first hospital, built in 1929, displaying medical paraphernalia of earlier eras, and a restored 1850 stagecoach station. The Rio Grande Valley Museum is open Wednesday through Saturday from 10:00 a.m. to 4:00 p.m., Sunday from 1:00 to 4:00 p.m., closed Mondays and Tuesdays. Admission is free.
▲Laguna Atascosa National Wildlife Refuge—Once a part of the Rio Grande delta before the river changed course, this wetland across the Intracoastal Waterway from

South Padre Island is a popular birding spot in the late fall and winter months. Seasonal inhabitants include green jays, chachalacas, Canada and snow geese, black-bellied whistling ducks, and 80 percent of all redhead ducks in North America. Mammals include ocelots, coyotes, bobcats, and white-tailed deer. The refuge has a scenic drive and hiking trails. To get there, exit from US 77 just north of Harlingen and follow FM 106 east for 27 miles. Past the refuge, the road veers south to rejoin today's main route on TX 100 outside of Port Isabel. Laguna Atascosa is open all year during daylight hours, though the visitor center is only open from October to April, 10:00 a.m. to 4:00 p.m. daily. Admission is $2 per vehicle.

▲▲**South Padre Island**—The southern 5 miles are packed with resort development, but most of the island remains a strip of endless white beach, sand dunes, and subtropical flora. Seabirds and seashells are abundant. At the southern tip of the island is thoroughly developed Isla Blanca County Park, a convenient and sometimes busy place to sunbathe among the dunes. Among the park's attractions is the Pan American University Coastal Studies Laboratory, where you can take a self-guided tour and learn about life in the Gulf of Mexico Sunday through Thursday from 1:30 to 4:30 p.m., closed Fridays and Saturdays. The entrance fee to the park is $1 per vehicle; admission to the laboratory is free. North of town, less developed Andy Bowie County Park gives you access to the wilder part of the beach.

Camping

On South Padre Island, **Isla Blanca County Park** has 300 RV spaces and over 100 tent sites. Fees are $10 per night. The park has a restaurant, snack bar, grocery store, fishing pier, beachwear shop, laundry, showers, and plenty of pavement. South Padre Island is a very busy tourist resort in the height of the summer tourist season and on week-ends at any time of year, though business becomes so slow at other times that many shops and restaurants close during the winter months despite the near-perfect subtropical climate (water temperatures can be chilly).

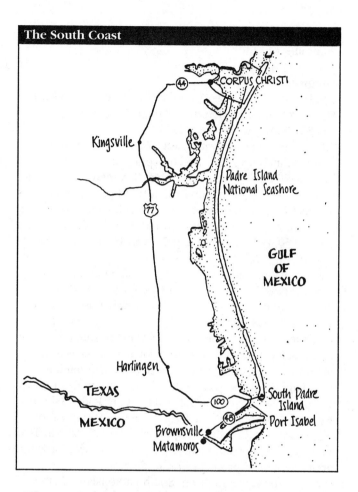

The South Coast

If you are planning a visit in the summer or on a Friday or Saturday evening, call ahead for reservations to the Cameron County Park System, (512) 761-5493. Reservations are accepted up to 15 days in advance. The park is located on the southern tip of the island. After crossing the Queen Isabella Causeway, turn right; you can't miss it.

If you turn left instead and go north on Padre Boulevard all the way through town, you will come to **Andy Bowie County Park**. Past this park's pedestrians-only area, you can drive on the beach and camp wherever you wish. There are no hookups, rest rooms,

drinking water, or other manmade amenities—just miles
and miles of sand.

Lodging

South Padre Island has several resort motels such as the
Holiday Inn Beach Resort (800-292-7506 in Texas,
800-531-7405 nationwide, $95 in spring and summer, $75
off-season) and the **South Padre Hilton Resort** (800-
292-7704 in Texas, $140 and up spring and summer, as
low as $90 off-season). At the **Best Western Fiesta Isles**
(210-761-4913), rooms run $108 to $118 in the summer, as
low as $48 from September through February. The lowest-
priced motel on South Padre Island, with in-season rates
below $50, is the basic, aging **Surf Motel** at 2612 Gulf
Boulevard, (210) 943-2831.

South Padre Island has more condominium units than
motel rooms, and most of them are for rent when the
owners are not using them. It is generally possible to rent
a condo for less than it would cost to stay in one of the
resort motels (rates start around $90 in the summer season,
under $60 off-season) and enjoy kitchen facilities as a
money-saving extra. Of nearly a dozen condominium
rental agencies operating in this little community of only
1,000 permanent residents, the largest are **Padre Island
Rentals** (800-292-7520 in Texas or 800-531-4540 nationwide) and **Sand Dollar Properties** (800-527-0294 in Texas
or 800-531-4541 nationwide). They will send you brochures
about individual properties on request.

Across the causeway from South Padre Island, at the
boat harbor in Port Isabel, is the **Yacht Club Hotel** at 700
Yturria, (210) 943-1301. Room rates at this historic 1926
hotel range from $35 to $50 for a double. Although the
yacht club was originally built for the wealthy, rooms are
quite small. Ask for one that opens onto the second-floor
veranda overlooking the harbor.

Food

While lodging may be more expensive along the beach,
restaurants on South Padre Island tend to be remarkably
affordable. The best view to be found at any of the

waterfront restaurants is at the steak-and-seafood **Jetties Restaurant** (943-6461) in Isla Blanca County Park, serving lunch and dinner daily. The fare is Tex-Mex and seafood, moderately priced.

Other popular island dining spots include **Blackbeard's**, 103 E. Saturn, 761-2962, serving hamburgers, sandwiches, and shrimp daily from 11:00 a.m. to 11:00 p.m., and **Callie's Kitchen**, 2412 Padre Boulevard, 943-5627, serving everything from barbecue to Mexican food—and, of course, seafood.

The dining room at the **Yacht Club** in Port Isabel, 700 Yturria, 943-1301, serves wonderfully prepared seafood dishes in an atmosphere of quaint elegance from 6:00 to 9:00 p.m. (closed Wednesdays). The prices, while higher than those at the other restaurants mentioned above, are less than you'd expect to pay.

A tiny place that serves the best breakfasts on South Padre Island all day (6:00 a.m. to 6:00 p.m., closed Sundays) is **Ro-Van's Restaurant and Bakery**, 5304 Padre Boulevard, 943-6972.

THE RIO GRANDE VALLEY

Today's route is the first leg of a journey up the Rio Grande along the U.S./Mexican border. The lower Rio Grande Valley was its own independent nation for two years in the mid-nineteenth century, and even today it is strikingly different from other parts of Texas. The reasons are reliably warm winter weather and proximity to the border. At the same latitude as Miami, Florida, the valley grows year-round vegetables, flowers, and citrus fruits—including the Texas ruby red grapefruit—and attracts a migratory population of "winter Texans," RV-driving refugees from cold northern climates. The valley has one of the poorest regional economies in the United States, while the other side of the river, which is poorer yet, is one of the most prosperous regions in Mexico. Undocumented workers from Mexico are a topic of continuing controversy in these parts. The borderline is as vague as the Rio Grande is muddy in this unique transition zone between two very different nations.

Suggested Schedule

9:00 a.m.	Visit South Padre Island's "Turtle Lady."
11:00 a.m.	Leave the island. Climb Port Isabel Lighthouse.
11:30 a.m.	Drive to Brownsville.
12:00 noon	Visit the Gladys Porter Zoo. Snack there. Later, see the Port of Brownsville. Or walk across the International Bridge to Matamoros.
3:00 p.m.	Drive the Military Highway along the Rio Grande, taking a break along the way at Santa Ana National Wildlife Refuge.
5:00 p.m.	Find a campsite at Bentsen-Rio Grande Valley State Park or spend the night in McAllen or Rio Grande City.

Travel Route: South Padre Island to Mission (90 miles)
Take TX 48 west for 24 miles to Brownsville. Cross the
bridge to Matamoros on foot or by taxi. Take US 281
(Military Highway) west from Brownsville for 55 miles to
Hidalgo, then go north on TX 336 for 7 miles to McAllen.
Get on US 83 westbound and drive for a few miles to the
adjoining town of Mission.

To get to Bentsen-Rio Grande Valley State Park from US
83 in Mission, take the Palmview exit. Turn west and
follow the signs on Farm Road 2062 and Park Road 43 for
about 5 miles to the park.

Sightseeing Highlights
▲▲**Sea Turtle, Inc.**—Ila Loetscher, the "Turtle Lady," is a
South Padre Island legend. She operates her home at 5805
Gulf Boulevard as a rehabilitation center for sick, injured,
or stranded sea turtles and works for reintroduction of the
Gulf of Mexico's endangered Kemp's ridley sea turtles,
which may become extinct by the year 2000. Funding for
these activities comes mainly from donations raised at her
"Meet the Turtles" shows, starring turtles who cannot
return to the open sea and have become permanent
residents of the center. Shows are Tuesday and Saturday
mornings at 9:00 a.m. during the summer months and
10:00 a.m. the rest of the year. Minimum donation
requested is $1. If you cannot be there for one of the
shows, a volunteer may be available to show you around
the facility anyway. Call 761-2544 to find out.
▲**Port Isabel Lighthouse State Historic Site**—Built in
1853, out of use since 1905, this is the only lighthouse on
the Texas coast that is open to the public. Climb the stair-
ways and short ladders to the glass-enclosed observation
deck on top and you'll be rewarded with a panoramic
view of Port Isabel, South Padre Island, and the Gulf. The
lighthouse is open daily from 10:00 to 5:00 p.m. Admission
is $1 for adults, 50 cents for children ages 6 to 12.
▲▲**Gladys Porter Zoo**—Brownsville's zoo, 2 miles north
of the city at 500 Ringgold Street, is reputed to be one of
the ten best in the nation, a fine example of what all zoos
should be like. It is a major participant in the international

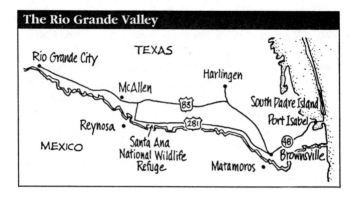

The Rio Grande Valley

endangered species captive breeding program for animals from Africa, Asia, Australia, and Latin America. Instead of being confined to cages, animals live on islands separated from humans by moats. The zoo is open Monday through Friday from 9:00 a.m. to 5:30 p.m., Saturdays and Sundays 9:00 a.m. to 6:00 p.m. Admission is $5 per adult, $2.50 for children ages 2 to 13, with a $1 per vehicle parking fee. A tour train takes visitors around the zoo on Sundays only for $1 per adult, 50 cents for children.

▲▲**International Bridge to Matamoros**—Matamoros, Mexico, across the Rio Grande from Brownsville, played a vital role in Texas history during the American Civil War. Cotton was the principal cash crop in Texas in those days, but during the Civil War, Union blockades made it all but impossible to sell cotton to overseas buyers. The United States could not blockade foreign ports, though, so growers from all over Texas (mostly women, children, and slaves, since the menfolk were elsewhere fighting the war) used to carry their cotton in wagons to the tip of Texas, where they floated the bales across the river to the free port of Matamoros. In fact, the city of Matamoros was a major port before its stateside suburb, Brownsville, was founded.

More than in most Texas towns along the Rio Grande, citizens on both sides of the border view the two cities as a single entity. The international bridge linking the two is right downtown where International Boulevard crosses the river. The toll to cross the bridge is 10 cents per person to

Matamoros and 20 cents returning to Brownsville; the toll for vehicles is 50 cents. A station for guided tours, a taxi stand, and a tourist information center (*se habla inglés*) dispensing city maps are located on the Mexican side of the bridge. Matamoros's main plaza is about a mile south of the bridge and a long block west at Guerrero and Calle 6. The public market is west of the Plaza at Guerrero and Calle 8. See How to Use this Book for more information on border crossings.

▲**Santa Ana National Wildlife Refuge**—Just south of US 281 near Hidalgo, this small refuge (200 acres) is considered one of the finest bird sanctuaries in the country. Especially known for doves, including several rare species, the forest is home to 370 bird species including 31 found only in the lower Rio Grande Valley, such as the kiskidee flycatcher and the green jay, and to tropical mammals like the ocelot and the jaguarundi. A 12-mile network of interconnecting trails makes exploring the refuge easy. Even easier is the interpretive tram (November through April only, $2 per adult, $1 for children under 12). The refuge is open year-round, Monday through Friday from 8:00 a.m. to 4:30 p.m., Saturday and Sunday from 9:00 a.m. to 4:30 p.m. Admission is $2 per adult, $1 for children under 12.

▲**Top Tex Packing Company**—Mission is the home of the ruby red grapefruit, the only citrus fruit unique to Texas. You can learn all about it on a trip through Top Tex's greenhouses, orchards, and sorting and packing plant. Located on Shary Road, north of town off Farm Road 1924, the company is open for free self-guided tours Monday through Friday from 9:00 a.m. to 5:00 p.m., Saturday and Sunday 9:00 a.m. to 3:00 p.m. Fresh fruit is for sale there, too.

▲**Bentsen-Rio Grande Valley State Park**—Nearly six hundred acres of the north bank of the Rio Grande south-west of Mission have been set aside as one of the last natural areas in the Rio Grande Valley. The riverside park is home to over 200 bird species including rarities like Audubon's oriole, the red-eye cowbird, and the zone-tail hawk. This is an ideal picnicking or camping spot. The day-use fee is $2 per vehicle.

▲**La Lomita Chapel**—Three miles south of town on Farm Road 1016 is the mission for which Mission, Texas, was named. The oldest mission church still in use in Texas, it was built in 1845 by the Oblate Fathers, who also brought the first citrus seeds to Texas. The small chapel is open during daylight hours. Admission is free. Nature trails are nearby.

▲**Los Ebanos Ferry**—West of Mission and 3 miles south on Farm Road 886, this is the last hand-operated ferry across the Mexican border. In the nineteenth century, ferries like this used to carry people, animals, and cargo across all the major rivers in Texas; Dallas got its start the same way. This ferry can carry two cars on each trip, but there's no reason for you to take yours. It only goes to a stand of ebony trees (the wood is used to make the black keys on pianos as well as other decorative items) and a dirt road that leads to the Mexican village of Diaz Ordaz. Pedestrians can ride but may be asked to earn their passage with brief physical labor helping pull the ferry across or grabbing dock ropes. Daily hours of operation are 8:00 a.m. to 4:00 p.m.

Lodging

Numerous hotel and motel possibilities present themselves along US 83 in McAllen (pop. 84,000) and Mission (pop. 29,000). The 1920s-vintage **San Juan Hotel**, at 125 West Business 83 in the little town of San Juan, 3 miles east of McAllen, has been completely restored and has air conditioning and a pool. Rates run $26 to $35. For reservations, call (210) 781-5339. At the **Mission Inn**, situated where Business Route 83 rejoins US 83, room rates start at $33 a night with cable television, in-room phones, and a pool. Call (210) 581-7451.

Travelers seeking unusual accommodations might continue beyond Mission on US 83 for another 40 miles to Rio Grande City, established at the end of the nineteenth century when riverboats plied the Rio Grande picking up crops to carry down to the port at Brownsville/Matamoros. This town was the farthest point upriver where the boats stopped and turned around. Its single tourist attraction today is a replica of the Grotto of Lourdes in France. The **LaBorde House**, 601 E. Main Street, Rio Grande City, TX 78582, (210) 487-5101, is an 1899 historic hotel with just eight rooms at about $60 a night double including continental breakfast.

Camping

The many privately operated RV parks in the McAllen/ Mission area, often shaded by citrus groves, cater primarily to long-term "winter Texans." By far the best camping in these parts for natural surroundings is at **Bentsen-Rio Grande Valley State Park**, where campsites range from $4 for unimproved tent sites to $10 for RV sites with full hookups.

Food

Away from the coast, the regional cuisine of the Rio Grande Valley is Tex-Mex—authentic versions of the "Mexican" food you're used to back home as well as more local specialities such as fajitas, strips of barbecued beef in a chili sauce. Among many hole-in-the-wall possibilities, try low-priced **La Casa del Taco** in McAllen at 1100 Houston, open daily from 8:00 a.m. to 10:00 p.m., Saturday until 12:00 midnight. McAllen also has three **Luby's Cafeterias**—off US 83 at 500 N. Jackson Road and in the Town & Country and Gateway shopping centers—making McAllen one of your more sophisticated dining-out towns for this part of the state. All three are open from 10:45 a.m. to 8:00 p.m.

LAREDO AND SAN ANTONIO

Today's itinerary involves a long drive from the Rio Grande Valley to San Antonio in the center of Texas, across one of the emptiest areas of the state, with a midday intermission at Laredo. The capital of the Republic of the Rio Grande during its brief bid for independence 150 years ago, Laredo (pop. 110,000) is the most Mexican of Texas towns, with a 90 percent Hispanic population, virtually part of the same city as Nuevo Laredo, Mexico.

In 1989, *Places Rated Almanac*'s annual survey of the "Most Livable Cities" in the United States ranked Laredo number 331 out of 333—one of the least livable places anywhere based on survey criteria such as climate, public transportation, crime, education, health care, jobs, and the arts. Though some folks might not want to live there, Laredo is a great place to visit thanks to its unique history and predominantly Mexican culture.

Suggested Schedule

9:00 a.m.	Leave the McAllen/Mission area.
11:30 a.m.	Arrive in Laredo. Visit the Museum of the Republic of the Rio Grande.
12:30 p.m.	Stroll across International Bridge I to Nuevo Laredo, Mexico.
1:30 p.m.	Lunch in old Mexico.
3:00 p.m.	Walk back to the United States, return to your vehicle, and head north on the interstate.
5:00 p.m.	Arrive in San Antonio. Check into your accommodations. (Campers will want to detour from the interstate to camp by the lake at Choke Canyon and visit San Antonio tomorrow morning.)

Travel Route: Mission to San Antonio (285 miles)
Follow US 83 all the way from Mission to Laredo, a distance of 130 miles through Texas brush country, including

a big "oil patch." At Laredo, get on I-35 and drive north for 155 fast miles to San Antonio.

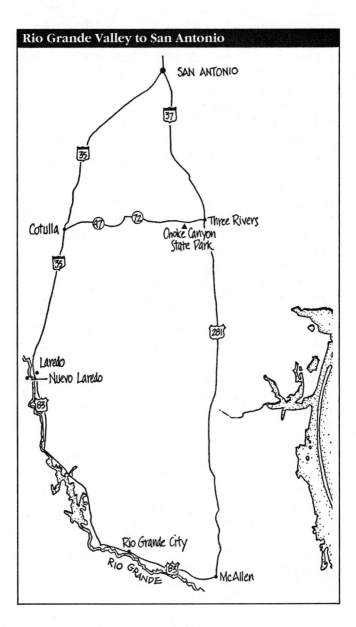

Rio Grande Valley to San Antonio

Sightseeing Highlights

▲▲**Museum of the Republic of the Rio Grande**—From 1839 to 1841, while Mexico and the Republic of Texas fought over the issue of which river formed the border between the two countries, the sparse population of the Rio Grande Valley on both sides of the river tried to settle the dispute by forming a separate nation, the Republic of the Rio Grande, with Laredo as its capital. The republic failed to win recognition from other nations (maybe diplomats from foreign capitals were reluctant to be stationed in remote Laredo), and the land north of the river was annexed to the United States along with the rest of Texas. You can learn about the region's brief period of independence at the museum in the Republic of the Rio Grande Building, downtown at 1050 Zaragoza Street on San Agustin Plaza. The museum is open Tuesday through Sunday from 10:00 a.m. to 4:00 p.m., closed Mondays. Donations are appreciated.

▲▲**Nuevo Laredo, Mexico**—Two international bridges a few blocks apart run between Laredo, Texas, and Nuevo Laredo, Mexico. International Bridge II is the south end of I-35, an easy route for those crossing the border by car. For pedestrians, the better route is International Bridge I, a block west and two blocks south of San Agustin Plaza and the museum. After crossing the bridge (15 cents apiece for pedestrians or 75 cents per vehicle), you'll immediately find yourself in the city's main public market. For information on border crossings, see "How to Use This Book."

Food

Pushcart food vendors and little cafés make **City Hall Square**, Laredo's cool and charming central plaza area, an inviting place to dine outdoors. Make a dinner of seafood, fresh bread, and tropical fruit under the big, shady oaks in the courtyard. Enter the square from San Agustin Street downtown.

Good Tex-Mex food at affordable prices can be found at **Taco Palenque**, 4515 San Bernardo in Laredo, Texas, with both drive-through and sit-down service 24 hours a day, seven days a week. Try enchiladas smothered in mole, a popular Mexican sauce made of peanuts, chocolate, and chili powder. Sounds strange, tastes great.

Many of the best Laredo restaurants are on the Nuevo Laredo, Mexico, side of the border. For regional specialties from all over Mexico such as Yucatán-style chicken and roast goat, eat at **Victoria 3020** on the corner of Victoria and Matamoros, not far from the south end of International Bridge I. (There are also streets named Victoria and Matamoros in downtown Laredo, but they do not intersect and are unrelated to the streets of the same name on the Mexican side.) This is one of Nuevo Laredo's more expensive restaurants; prices are moderate by U.S. standards. Victoria 3020 is open daily from 11:00 a.m. to 11:00 p.m.

A lower-priced place in Mexico where you can sip margaritas and dine on barbecued goat in a quiet patio setting is **Mexico Tipico** on Guerrero Street about a mile south of International Bridge I. Hours vary.

See tomorrow's listings for restaurant and nightclub suggestions in San Antonio.

Lodging

San Antonio is a popular convention city, and the room rates at most chain hotels and motor inns here are among the highest in the state. But there are some interesting alternatives.

Just across the street from the Alamo, within easy walking distance of the River Walk, is the **Crockett Hotel**, 320 Bonham Street, (210) 225-6500. This historic 1909 hotel looks old on the outside, but inside it has been completely restored. Guest rooms are modern, and there is a sunny central atrium with a courtyard café. Rates for two range from $95 to $125.

Nearby, the **Emily Morgan Hotel at Alamo Plaza**, 705 E. Houston, (210) 225-8486, is an elegant restoration of a 1930s office building. Room rates are $99 a night. (Like the Crockett, the Emily Morgan is named after a hero of the Texas War for Independence, though she is unknown to most non-Texans. Miss Morgan, a mulatto or "high yellow" slave girl, kept Mexican General Santa Anna distracted during his siesta on April 21, 1836, as Texan General Sam Houston invaded the Mexican camp, captured Santa Anna with his pants down, and won the Battle of San Jacinto. Santa Anna was given his freedom in exchange for Texas independence, and Emily Morgan, Texas's first female war hero, was immortalized in song as "The Yellow Rose of Texas.")

Situated next to the Rivercenter shopping area on the River Walk and across from the Alamo at 204 Alamo Plaza, the historic **Menger Hotel** dates back to 1859. Generals Robert E. Lee and Ulysses S. Grant stayed here. So did former Republic of Texas President Sam Houston, Sarah Bernhardt, and President Theodore Roosevelt. New additions have been built on since then, expanding the hotel to over 350 rooms. You can make a special request to stay in the hotel's "Authentic 19th-Century Wing" when you call for reservations. The number is (210) 228-0022. Rates range from $118 to $138.

The **Norton-Brackenridge Bed and Breakfast Inn** is located six blocks from downtown, within easy walking distance of the River Walk, at 230 Madison Street. It is a finely restored turn-of-the-century house with antique furnishings and polished pine floors. All five guest rooms have private entrances and queen- or king-size beds. Rates range from $70 to $90 a night. Reservations are required. Call (210) 271-3442. The **Riverwalk Inn**, on the Riverwalk at 329 Old Guilbeau Street, (210) 229-9922, offers 11 luxuriously rustic guestrooms in five two-story log homes built in Tennessee in the 1840s and moved to downtown San Antonio by innkeepers Jan and Tracy Hammer in 1994. A 75-foot-long porch overlooks the Riverwalk. Rates range from $89 to $169. The **Bullis House**, near Fort Sam Houston at 621 Pierce Street, (210) 223-9426, is a white Greek revival mansion originally built in 1906 for U.S. Army General Bullis and now restored as a country inn and International Youth Hostel. Private bedrooms with shared bath are a bargain in the $40 range for two; breakfast costs $3 per person extra. Reservations are essential. You can book a room at these or a half-dozen other San Antonio bed and breakfasts through **Bed & Breakfast Texas Style** (see Day 2).

Camping

There is no public campground close to San Antonio or anywhere else along today's travel route. If you're traveling by RV and wish to spend the night in the city, your best bet is the huge **Alamo KOA Kampground** near I-35 on the east side of town. Sites cost about $16 a night. Call 224-9296 for directions to get there.

A more relaxing plan for campers is to modify the suggested travel route as follows: 68 miles north of Laredo, exit I-35 at Cotulla and drive east on TX 97 and TX 72 for about 50 miles to Choke Canyon Reservoir. (Tomorrow, continue east on TX 72 to I-37 and turn north to San Antonio, a 75-mile drive.) There are two **Choke Canyon State Park** campgrounds along the lakeshore, both just off TX 72. The more developed is the Calliham Unit, which has a grocery store and restaurant, tennis courts, and nature trails, with forty campsites. There are more campsites but fewer facilities at the South Shore Unit, about 8 miles farther east. Camping fees at both units are $9 a night. Both offer water and electric hookups and are open year-round.

SAN ANTONIO

This is the place where Texas got its start, in more ways than one. The site of modern-day San Antonio was first settled in the early 1700s by Spanish missionaries. You can still find the original mission churches along the riverbank, some of them tucked away behind suburban housing tracts. A century later, one of the old missions, the Alamo, was the scene of a series of incidents that touched off the Texas War for Independence. No exploration of Texas would be complete without a visit to this most sacred historic site in the state. Afterward, enjoy a leisurely stroll along downtown San Antonio's unique River Walk.

Suggested Schedule	
9:00 a.m.	Visit the Alamo.
10:30 a.m.	Take a walk along the River Walk. Shop, ride the water taxi, and visit historic La Villita.
12:30 p.m.	Lunch along the River Walk.
2:00 p.m.	Follow the Mission Trail to the other four old Spanish missions in San Antonio (or visit Sea World of Texas).
Evening	Dinner and nightlife on the River Walk.

San Antonio

San Antonio (pop. 940,000) can be the most confusing of all Texas cities to drive around in. Freeways become entangled, change course abruptly, or end in construction detours. In the downtown area, streets run in haphazard directions, always one way (usually the wrong way). Like Houston, San Antonio has a 40-mile loop freeway (I-410, known as the Parkway) surrounding the city. But since San Antonio is only a fraction of Houston's size, the loop skirts the outer edge of the city, providing convenient access to several military bases but not to much of interest to civilian sightseers.

For maximum enjoyment on a visit to San Antonio, find your way to downtown (the only cluster of skyscrapers in this sprawling city), park at any of several lots near the Alamo, and spend the day on foot. Most of the major points of interest are downtown within the area bounded by interstates 10, 35, and 37. The Alamo is west of the Commerce Street/Convention Center exit from I-35/37, which flanks the east side of downtown.

Sightseeing Highlights

▲▲**The Alamo**—The most famous historic site in Texas, this Spanish mission was built in 1744 by Franciscan monks. About eighty years later, when Mexicans won their independence from Spain and banished the Franciscans, the Alamo was abandoned. It was being used as a Mexican military garrison in early 1836 when a citizens' uprising drove the army out of town and seized the old mission, cannons and all. Unfortunately, the majority of the Texan rebels had left town to join Sam Houston's army, leaving just a small force to defend the Alamo, when Mexican General Santa Anna arrived with a force of soldiers that outnumbered the Texans 12 to 1. After laying siege to the Alamo for 13 days, Santa Anna's troops stormed the walls, sustained huge losses (eight times as many Mexicans as Texans died in the fighting), massacred the defenders, and executed the few survivors. The slaughter at the Alamo shocked Anglo settlers across Texas into a revolutionary fervor, and a month later Texas won its independence from Mexico.

A film produced by the Daughters of the Republic of Texas, shown regularly in a small room adjoining the museum, recounts the heroism of Travis, Crockett, Bowie, and the other Alamo defenders. The museum contains artifacts of the battle, including Jim Bowie's knife and Davy Crockett's rifle, Old Betsy. Equally heroic in its own way is the story of how a few preservationists in the early twentieth century fought to save the crumbling ruins of the Alamo from urban redevelopment that would have replaced it with a bank building. The landscaped grounds

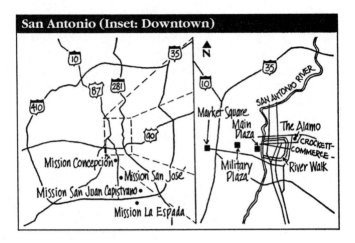

San Antonio (Inset: Downtown)

of the Alamo complex invite quiet contemplation in the shadow of the city's skyscrapers. And the old mission church, the largest building in the Alamo complex? It's a souvenir shop.

The Alamo is open Monday through Saturday from 9:00 a.m. to 5:30 p.m., Sundays 10:00 a.m. to 5:30 p.m. Admission is free.

▲▲River Walk (Paseo del Rio)—The San Antonio River, meandering in a 1-mile loop through the center of downtown, has become San Antonio's most distinctive landmark. Until recently, the river posed an obstacle to orderly urban planning, and the old, run-down buildings along its banks were eyesores. The U.S. Army Corps of Engineers failed in attempts to divert it and fill it in, and finally the city decided to undertake a unique urban renewal project— changing the river into a Texan's vision of Venice. Today, the river is lined with subtropical flora and new and restored Mediterranean-style buildings containing trendy Mexican restaurants, frozen yogurt shops, "Santa Fe style" galleries, boutiques, nightclubs, and hotels, but it feels parklike. You can stroll along the River Walk from practically any place to any other place in the downtown area without ever hearing traffic noise, or you can travel in style on a "river taxi," a small motorized passenger barge. The fare is $3 for adults, $1 for children under 4 feet tall.

The boats run at 10-minute intervals from 9:00 a.m. to
10:30 p.m. during the summer months, 10:00 a.m. to 8:00
p.m. the rest of the year.

Just a few blocks from the Alamo, at Rivercenter Mall
on the River Walk, an IMAX theater shows a 45-minute
dramatization, *The Alamo: The Price of Freedom*, on a six-
story-high wraparound screen. Admission is $6.25 per
adult, $3.95 for children ages 3 to 11. Call 225-4629 for
show times.

La Villita, the one-block historic district adjoining the
River Walk and bounded by S. Alamo, S. Presa, and Nueva
streets, preserves the oldest surviving residences in San
Antonio. It was here that General Cos (Santa Anna's
brother-in-law) made his home and surrendered San
Antonio (including the Alamo) to Texan rebels, setting the
stage for the famous battle. A slum fifty years ago, La Villita
has been gentrified and made more "authentic" to become
a combination historical park and arts-and-crafts district.
Banana trees and bougainvilleas shade art galleries and the
Conservation Society's Old San Antonio Museum. La Villita
is open daily from 10:00 a.m. to 6:00 p.m. Admission
is free.

A short distance from La Villita but on the other side of
the river is the Hertzberg Circus Collection, a free museum
in the San Antonio Public Library annex which is a perfect
pause for visitors with children. Amid the big top paraphernalia is a complete miniature circus. The collection is
open Monday through Saturday from 9:00 a.m. to 5:00 p.m.
and Sundays from May through October 1:00 to 5:00 p.m.
Admission is $2 per person.

The eastern spur of the River Walk, which parallels
Market Street to the convention center, takes you to the
Hemisfair Plaza area, site of the 1968 World's Fair, where
you'll find the 622-foot Tower of the Americas with the
best view around of San Antonio and the southern Hill
Country (the elevator to the observation deck costs $2.50
for adults, $1.25 for senior citizens, and $1 for children
ages 4 to 12) as well as two fascinating museum exhibits
about the city's past—the Institute of Texas Cultures (open
Tuesday through Sunday 9:00 a.m. to 5:00 p.m., closed

Mondays, admission by donation) and the Mexican
Cultural Institute, where a museum of Latin American art is
part of the only accredited National University of Mexico
extension on U.S. soil (open Tuesday through Friday from
9:00 a.m. to 5:30 p.m., Saturdays and Sundays from 11:00
a.m. to 5:00 p.m., free admission).

To reach the River Walk from the Alamo, walk south
from Alamo Plaza to Crockett Street and half a block west
to the intersection with Broadway, where you'll find a
stairway down to the river

▲**Main Plaza and Military Plaza**—This historic part of
downtown San Antonio is not along the River Walk, but
it is within walking distance. On the west side of the
downtown area between Commerce and Dolorosa streets
bounded by Cameron and Soledad, Main Plaza and
Military Plaza formed the heart of the town during Spanish
colonial times and still serve as the center of government;
the modern city hall and county courthouse stand along-
side buildings that date back to the eighteenth century.

Churches have occupied the site of San Francisco
Cathedral on the west side of Main Plaza since 1738, when
a group of immigrants from the Canary Islands who were
not accepted by the congregation at Mission San Antonio
de Valero (the Alamo) began work on a small parish
church here. It took twenty years to complete and stood
for more than a century before the new, much larger
cathedral was built around it. A plaque on the cathedral
perpetuates the doubtful legend that the heroes of the
Alamo are buried in the churchyard.

Military Plaza was originally a Spanish army drill field.
After Texas independence, the plaza became a public
market, the busiest place in San Antonio for fifty years until
construction of the new courthouse forced vendors to
relocate to Market Square. The **Spanish Governors'
Palace**, on the west side of Military Plaza, is the city's only
surviving Spanish colonial aristocrat's home, now restored
by the San Antonio Conservation Society with eighteenth-
century handmade furnishings and decor. Elegant touches
contrast oddly with other features that hint at crude living
conditions on the frontier, so that the Spanish Governors'

Palace evokes a more vivid impression of Spanish colonial ways than any other historic site in the city. The palace is open Monday through Saturday from 9:00 a.m. to 5:00 p.m., Sundays 10:00 a.m. to 5:00 p.m. Admission is $1 for adults, 50 cents for children ages 7 to 12.

▲**Market Square**—Several blocks farther west on Commerce or Dolorosa from the Main Plaza and Military Plaza, between Santa Rosa and I-35, this public market-place has been used by the city's Mexican community for over 100 years. Market Square as seen today is the result of a 1976 urban renewal project; before that, it went under the name of Haymarket Square. To buy fresh produce at the farmer's market, you'll want to arrive bright and early in the morning. El Mercado, the traditional Mexican market, is open 24 hours a day. Also at Market Square are the restored Market House, containing specialty shops, and the Market House Annex, housing the Centro de Artes del Mercado, the arts and crafts center. Concerts and fiestas often enliven the central mall on weekends. Both restaurants and pushcart vendors make Market Square the place to go for low-priced, authentic Mexican food.

▲▲**San Antonio Missions National Historical Park**— The four other mission churches besides the Alamo which survive from Spanish colonial times are at 2-mile intervals along the San Antonio River south of downtown. To visit them, follow St. Mary's south to Mission Road. First visit Mission Concepción, at the corner of Mission Road and Mitchell Street, where you can pick up a National Park Service map that will lead you to the others, all on suburban side streets off Mission Road. Admission is free to all four missions, open daily from 9:00 a.m. to 6:00 p.m. during daylight saving months, 8:00 a.m. to 5:00 p.m. the rest of the year.

Each mission contains exhibits on a different theme assigned by the National Park Service. Mission Concepción (Nuestra Señora de la Purisima Concepción de Acuña) dates back to 1731, making it the oldest unrestored church in the United States that is still being used as a church. It carries the theme, "The Mission as a Religious Center." Original frescoes painted by Franciscan monks and Indians in the eighteenth century are still visible on the interior walls. Mission San Jose, with its graceful archwork and flying buttresses and its elaborately crafted Rose Window, was originally established in 1720 and extensively restored in the 1930s. Its theme is "The Mission as Social Center and as a Center of Defense." Mission San Juan Capistrano, established in 1731, carries the theme, "The Mission as Economic Center." Of special interest are antique images of Christ and the Virgin Mary made of cornstalk pith and dating back to the mid-eighteenth century, as well as an unusual figure of St. John of Capistrano, a fifteenth-century crusade leader, in full armor, standing victorious over the body of an infidel. Mission San Francisco de la Espada was established here in 1731 by a group of nuns who moved their mission from the forests of East Texas, where they had spent the past ten years. Its theme is "The Mission as Vocational Education Center." The nearby aqueduct that served the mission is the only Spanish aqueduct in the United States. At Mission San Francisco de la Espada, you are near the southern portion of I-410, the loop parkway that surrounds the city.

▲▲**Sea World of Texas**—The world's largest marine life theme park fills 250 acres on the western edge of San Antonio. Here you'll find Sea World's superstar, Shamu the orca, or killer whale (there's one at each Sea World park around the country, and they all have the same name), along with her baby orca, born in early 1993. There are also beluga whales, dolphins, seals, walruses, otters, birds, and water skiers. The whale and dolphin touching pool lets visitors and cetaceans experience each other up close, and an aquarium re-creates a South Pacific coral reef environment. Except for the History Walk, there's nothing particularly Texan about this popular tourist attraction landlocked more than 100 miles from the nearest seashore, but it's an ideal place to unleash children when they start to fidget from too many San Antonio historical sites. To get there, take I-410 West to the Westside Expressway (TX 151) northbound, then exit west on Westover Hills Boulevard, which takes you directly to the main gate. Sea World is open daily from 10:00 a.m. to 10:00 p.m. during

the summer months and on Saturdays and Sundays from
10:00 a.m. to 7:00 p.m. during the spring and fall months.
523-3611 or 800-422-SWTX for the current schedule). Allow
at least half a day to get your money's worth from the stiff
all-inclusive admission charge—$25.93 per adult, $17.27 for
children ages 3 to 11 and senior citizens.

Lodging and Camping

Noncampers, spend a second night at your San Antonio
hotel, motel, or bed and breakfast. Since there is no public
camping around San Antonio, campers may wish to drive
north to Austin tonight instead of tomorrow morning and
stay at McKinney Falls State Park on the south edge of that
city. See Day 12 for details.

Food

The River Walk is lined with restaurants, from charming
little sidewalk cafés to ritzy places offering expensive
continental haute cuisine. The following restaurants,
though some of them have addresses reflecting their street
level entrances, are all on the River Walk. An inexpensive
café and popular local hangout is **Big Bend** at 511 River
Walk, 225-4098. Other informal places that won't dent your
budget badly include German-style **Schilo's Delicatessen**
at 424 E. Commerce, 223-6692, closed Sundays, and the
nearby **Original Mexican Restaurant**, 415 E. Commerce,
224-9951. All three serve breakfast, lunch, and dinner. You
might also want to check out the **Calico Cat Tearoom**, a
salad, quiche, and pastry place at 306 N. Presa, 226-4925,
lunch only, closed Sundays. The **Rio Rio Cantina** at 421
E. Commerce, 226-8462, is a moderately priced restaurant
serving Mexican-nouveau dishes such as a *tostada pachuga
de pollo* packed with broiled chicken breast strips, avocado,
beans, tomato, and cheese. Under the same ownership, the
Zuñi Grill, 511 River Walk, 227-0864, serves creative
southwestern food, with an intriguing lunchtime soup and
salad selection. Try the nachos with duck sauce.

An exclusive restaurant worth the splurge is **Las
Canarias** in La Mansion del Rio Hotel. The name honors
immigrants from the Canary Islands who were among San

Antonio's early settlers. The cuisine is predominantly Spanish (not Mexican); try the paella. Las Canarias is especially worthy of your consideration on Saturday evenings, when flamenco dancers perform. It is only open for dinner Monday through Saturday and brunch on Sunday. Reservations are a good idea—call 225-4000.

Nightlife
Wander along the River Walk any evening and you'll have no trouble finding late-night hot spots, though rock 'n' roll is a rarity in this popular nightclub district. **The Landing** in the Hyatt Regency is a first-class jazz spot, while **Durty Nelly's** in the Hilton Palacio del Rio delivers old favorite sing-along piano music. At **Big Bend** (see Food above), there's no live music; late-night entertainment consists of good views of the River Walk and an eclectic mix of patrons, a perfect combination for relaxed people-watching.

AUSTIN

Austin is the capital of Texas, the main campus of the University of Texas, and the musical mecca of the Southwest. Today you'll have a chance to explore all three aspects of this upbeat, fast-growing city, and perhaps also visit one of the large, lovely parks that surround it.

Suggested Schedule

9:00 a.m.	Leave San Antonio.
10:30 a.m.	Arrive in Austin. Visit the state capitol building and the historical museums in the Old Land Office Building.
12:00 noon	Lunch.
1:00 p.m.	See the Lyndon Baines Johnson Library.
2:30 p.m.	Stroll around the University of Texas campus.
4:00 p.m.	How about a late afternoon picnic in Zilker Park?
Evening	Check out the nightlife along Sixth Street.

Travel Route: San Antonio to Austin (81 miles)
Follow I-35 north from San Antonio to Austin. Finding your way around Austin is easy, since most major sights—the capitol, the LBJ Library, the university, and the Sixth Street nightclub zone—are within a short distance west of I-35, the city's principal freeway. Just follow the signs.

Austin
Founded in 1839 at the dawn of Texas independence and named for Stephen F. Austin, who had established the first *norteamericano* settlement in Texas just 18 years before, Austin has grown to a present-day population of 750,000. About 10 percent of all Austin residents are students at the University of Texas, making Austin the contemporary music center of the Southwest and the only place in the state where it's generally regarded as okay to be gay or

lesbian, an aging hippie, a conceptual artist, or even (gasp!) an intellectual.

As the state capital, Austin is also at least part-time home to large numbers of politicians—flamboyant, fast on their feet, and frequently feminine—as well as a huge infrastructure of bureaucrats and the state's highest concentration of lawyers. And why not? Larger than the majority of the world's independent nations, Texas is the only U.S. state with the right by treaty with the federal government to secede from the United States whenever its people want to, or to divide itself into up to five states. A nation within a nation, Texas calls for a lot of governing, and Austin is where they do it.

Austin's recent rapid growth is due mainly to high-tech companies locating factories or research facilities in the area. Nicknamed "Silicon Gulch," the city has emerged as a major microelectronics and bioengineering center thanks to such attractive liveability factors as its sunbelt climate and its huge university. Not to mention the bats.

From mid-spring to mid-fall, Austin hosts three-quarters of a million Mexican freetail bats—one for every human resident. The nightly spectacle as the bats head out from their homes under the bridges that cross the Colorado River (widened through the city by a small dam and called Town Lake) rivals the more famous bat flight at Carlsbad Caverns (Day 19). Austin folks like their bats just fine, thanks; they've adopted them as unofficial city mascots. The bats eat ten tons of mosquitoes every night, thereby keeping thousands of gallons of Texas blood right where it belongs. Sunset batwatching is best by the Congress Street Bridge at Lamar Park, on the riverbank due south of downtown.

Sightseeing Highlights
▲▲▲**Lyndon Baines Johnson Library**—Some non-Texans may recall Lyndon Johnson as an unpopular president ("Hey, hey, L-B-J, how many kids did you kill today?"), his Great Society legacy of civil rights, Medicare, education, antipoverty, and highway beautification legislation overshadowed by the Vietnam War. But don't

even think of uttering any disparaging words about Lyndon Johnson in these parts, where he is commonly regarded as the greatest Texan of the twentieth century. To rediscover Johnson, visit the presidential library on the University of Texas campus, where he spent his last years teaching. You'll venture deeper into his world tomorrow in the Hill Country west of Austin.

The ground floor of the library is a museum of LBJ memorabilia, from young Lyndon's fourth-grade report card, to a vivid letter written by first lady Lady Bird Johnson on her first visit to Big Bend National Park, to a video of the president telling funny stories. The picture of the late president that emerges from these exhibits is warmer, friendlier, more personal than the one remembered in the cold glare of history. One exhibit does recount the unfortunate matter of Vietnam, suggesting that Johnson was misled into making that mistake by his advisers (presumably non-Texans).

Presidential papers from the Johnson administration (1963-1968) fill four stories of the library in floor-to-ceiling shelves of identical red file boxes, each bearing the presidential seal. You can see this astonishing volume of paperwork—35 million pages—through windows from the atrium where you catch the elevator.

On the top floor of the library is a replica of the Oval Office as it appeared in the Johnson era. The president kept abreast of world events using a tickertape machine and three TV sets—one for each network—which he watched simultaneously. Also on the top floor is a delightful collection of presidential campaign paraphernalia.

The Lyndon Baines Johnson Library and adjacent parking lot are located on the University of Texas campus at 2313 Red River near East 23rd Street. It is not far from I-35, and large signs make it easy to find from the interstate. It is open from 9:00 a.m. to 5:00 p.m. daily. Admission is free.

▲▲**University of Texas**—The Republic of Texas established the university in 1839 with a 115,000-acre land grant. The university did not decide on a location (Austin was chosen by popular vote in 1881), erect buildings, or open its doors to students until more than forty years later.

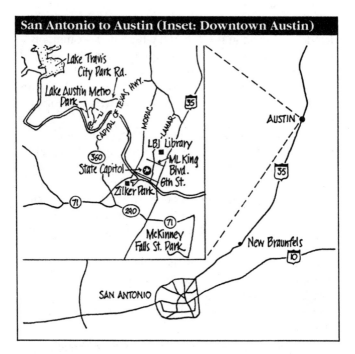

San Antonio to Austin (Inset: Downtown Austin)

In the 1920s, oil was discovered beneath the university's land grant acreage. The well, Santa Rita No. 1, generated $1.75 billion for the school's Permanent University Fund. The rig used to drill Santa Rita No. 1 was moved to Austin for public display and can be seen at the corner of Trinity and Martin Luther King Boulevard, midway between the campus and the capitol. Today, the University of Texas at Austin has about 45,000 students and ranks among the wealthiest higher education institutions in the nation. The constant supply of new graduates has been the biggest cause of Austin's rapid growth in recent years, drawing a parade of microelectronic and bioengineering firms to the city.

Leave your vehicle at the LBJ Library parking lot, since parking spaces are hard to find anywhere else in the university district. Detailed visitor information and campus maps are available at Sid Richardson Hall just south of the LBJ Library. Sid Richardson Hall houses the Barker Texas History Center, the largest collection in existence of historical documents about Texas. It is a closed-stack library, but changing exhibits are open to the public Monday through Saturday from 8:00 a.m. to 5:00 p.m. Admission is free.

West of the LBJ Library at 24th Street and Trinity is the Texas Memorial Museum, with four floors of exhibits on natural history, geology, archaeology, and anthropology. On the ground floor is the original Goddess of Liberty statue, a replica of which now graces the dome of the state capitol building. The museum is open Monday through Friday from 9:00 a.m. to 5:00 p.m., Saturday from 1:00 to 5:00 p.m. Admission is free.

The Texas Union, at 24th Street and Guadalupe, is the campus social center and the place to find information on current happenings at the university. Computer terminals show event lists continuously.

The Texas Tower, the university's landmark 27-story administration building, is visible from virtually any spot on campus, and its 68-bell carillon chimes every quarter-hour.

At the southwest corner of the campus, the Harry Ransom Center at 21st Street and Guadalupe contains the Huntington Art Gallery and Humanities Research Center. Exhibits include 300 paintings from author James A. Michener's American art collection, as well as Greek and Roman sculpture, western art works, photographs, and a rare Gutenberg Bible printed in 1455. The center is open Monday through Saturday from 9:00 a.m. to 5:00 p.m., Sundays from 1:00 to 5:00 p.m. There is no admission charge.

The commercial University District along Guadalupe has the most complete bookstores you're likely to encounter anywhere in Texas. At the University Coop Bookstore, the general interest books on the second floor include a generous selection of Texiana.

▲▲**State Capitol**—Texas has the largest state capitol building in the country. Although it is not quite as large as the United States Capitol, it is taller by seven feet. Looking up at the top of the dome from outside, notice the tower on which the statue stands—just tall enough to be the tallest. When construction started on the capitol building in

1882, the plan called for readily available, easy-to-quarry Austin limestone, but it proved useless for exterior work. Instead, stonecutters mined Granite Mountain, about 20 miles north of Johnson City (Day 13) or 50 miles from Austin. Cutting the pink granite blocks was slow work. It took 15,000 rail car loads to bring all those blocks down to Austin. Inside, the capitol building is even larger than it looks from the outside. Stop at the visitors desk in the south foyer to pick up a self-guiding tour pamphlet or join one of the free tours that run every 15 minutes from 8:30 a.m. to 4:30 p.m. daily.

On display throughout the capitol you'll find paintings of former governors and a marble bust of Texas's first woman governor as well as statues of heroes and copies of documents whereby Texas declared its independence from Mexico and seceded from the United States. Notice the "Seal of the Nations" design in terrazzo on the rotunda floor. The seal of the Republic of Texas is in the center; at the five points of the Texas star are the seals or coats of arms of the five other nations that have flown their flags on Texas soil—Spain, Mexico, France, the Confederacy, and the United States. Don't miss the view of the rotunda from the seventh-level balcony. Located at 11th and Congress just north of downtown (take the 11th Street exit from I-35; look for parking several blocks north of the capitol building on Congress). The capitol building is open daily from 6:00 a.m. to 11:00 p.m. Admission is free.

South of the capitol on 11th Street is the Old Land Office Building, designed in old-world style by a German immigrant architect in 1857. It houses two museums of historical relics from nineteenth-century Texas—the Daughters of the Confederacy Museum on the ground floor and the Daughters of the Republic of Texas Museum on the second floor. Both are open Wednesday through Saturday from 10:00 a.m. to 4:00 p.m., Sunday 1:00 to 4:00 p.m., closed Mondays and Tuesdays. Admission is free.

About a block west of the Old Land Office Building is the Old Bakery and Emporium at 1006 Congress, dating back to 1876. It now provides space for Austin senior citizens to sell homemade bakery items and handicrafts.

The hospitality desk provides the friendliest and most complete tourist information service in town. Hours are 9:00 a.m. to 4:00 p.m. Monday through Friday; in the summer months and Christmas season, it is also open on Saturdays from 10:00 a.m. to 3:00 p.m.

Two blocks west of the Old Land Office Building at 11th Street and Colorado is the stately antebellum Governor's Mansion, the oldest structure in the capital complex. Here 36 Texas chief executives have lived in luxury. Free tours of the grounds and the six public rooms on the first floor start every 20 minutes from 10:00 a.m. to 12:00 noon, Monday through Friday.

▲▲**Zilker Park**—This city park west of downtown is Austin's largest and most beautifully landscaped, the site of 22-acre Zilker Gardens, with roses, Oriental landscaping, a Swedish settler's log cabin, and a meditation trail, and the nearby, larger Austin Nature Center, with exhibits on dinosaurs and regional flora and fauna as well as hiking trails through a 90-acre wild area. The gardens are open Monday through Friday from 9:00 a.m. to 4:30 p.m., Saturday and Sunday from 2:00 to 5:00 p.m., and the nature center daily from 8:00 a.m. to 5:00 p.m. Both are free. The park itself is open daily from 8:00 a.m. to sunset.

The most popular spot in Zilker Park on hot days is Barton Springs, a thousand-foot-long swimming pool created around a crystal-clear natural spring that remains at 68 degrees year-round but is open for swimming only from April through October.

Lodging
The heart of Texas politics, Austin has plenty of downtown hotels vying for recognition as *the* place to stay when visiting the capital. The place where Lyndon and Lady Bird Johnson used to stay is the **Driskill Hotel**, 604 Brazos, (512) 474-5911. This 1886 historic hotel offers elegant, exceptionally spacious rooms starting around $89 per night, and it is centrally located in the Sixth Street nightlife district. (If LBJ were alive today, though, he might switch allegiances to the contemporary **Four Seasons Austin**, 99 San Jacinto, 512-478-4500. Located on the shore of Town

Lake with its popular hiking and biking trail on the edge of downtown, the Four Seasons sets the standard for luxury accommodations in Austin. Rooms cost $152 to $180 per night.)

At the other end of the lodging spectrum, because of the university, Austin has more than its share of youth hostels. A $10 bill will buy a night of dormitory living, meals included, at the **21st Street Co-op** (American Youth Hostels), 707 W. 21st, (512) 476-1857, or at **Taos Hall** (AYH), 2612 Guadalupe, (512) 474-6905, both on the edge of the university campus. University accommodations are also available by the night for under $20 at **Goodall Wooten Dorm** (men only, 2112 Guadalupe, 512-472-1343) or **Newman Hall** (women only, 2026 Guadalupe, 512-476-0669).

The highest concentration of motels is south of downtown along I-35, especially around the Woodward Avenue and Ben White Boulevard exits. Typical rates are $40 to $50 per night.

The **Brook House**, a popular bed and breakfast in a 1920s home located near the university and the capitol at 609 W. 33rd Street, (512) 459-0534, offers private guest cottages. Rates run $70 to $80 a night. In the same neighborhood and price range, the **McCallum House** at 613 W. 32nd Street, (512) 451-6744, offers bed and breakfast accommodations in an antique-filled Victorian house.

Camping

The most popular public campground in the Austin area is **McKinney Falls State Park** on the south edge of the city. To get there, take I-35 to the Ben White Boulevard exit (TX 71) and drive east for about 4 miles to Bastrop (US 183), then south for about 4 miles. Turn right (west) on Scenic Loop Road, following the state park signs for 2 miles to the park. The two falls for which the park is named are often mere trickles, and both the falls and the creek are off-limits to bathers because of pollution problems, but the park has other charms. It was formerly the estate of a racehorse breeder. The ruins of the original ranch house and the horse trainer's cottage can still be seen, and the training track has been made into a pretty 4-mile-long hiking and biking path that loops through most of the park, amid vegetation that ranges from 5-foot-tall prickly pear cactus to creekside cypress and cedar. Armadillos are common. Watch for these strange nocturnal creatures scavenging around the campground at dusk and later. Campsites cost $8, with an extra $2 charge for electric hookup, and there is a separate campsite loop for tent campers. The campground fills up quickly on weekends and every night during the summer months.

Another attractive camping possibility is **Lake Austin Metropolitan Park** (sometimes called by its former name, Emma Long Metropolitan Park) west of the city. To get there from I-35, take either the Ben White Boulevard (US 290) exit on the south side of town or the Research Boulevard (US 183) exit on the north side and go west to Capital of Texas Highway (Loop 360), which skirts the extreme west edge of Austin. Less than a mile north of the bridge over Lake Austin, take Farm Road 2222 west and you will soon come to City Park Road. Several miles south on this road, you will reach the park, campground, and lake. Lake Austin does not look much like a lake, more like a wide river. Formed by a dam within the city limits which fills the Colorado River with much more water than it would otherwise contain, Lake Austin is nearly 30 meandering miles long but only about a quarter of a mile across at its widest point. Three miles of the lake form the southern boundary of the park. There are swimming beaches as well as high, sheer cliffs and bluffs offering fine views from elevations of a thousand feet above the city. Full-hookup campsites cost $11.

Food
The **Cactus Cafe and Bar** in the university's student union serves student food at student prices, but you don't have to be a student to eat there.

You can find any kind of cuisine you crave along West Sixth Street. Among the many possibilities are: **Hoffbrau**, 613 W. Sixth, 472-0822, open weekdays from 11:00 a.m. to 2:00 p.m. and 5:00 to 8:30 p.m., closed Saturdays and

Sundays, serving Texas beef German-style along with beer
in an unpretentious atmosphere; **Tejas Grill**, 1110 W.
Sixth, 478-5355, open daily until midnight, serving both
Tex-Mex and Cajun food; and **Olive's Gourmet Pizza**,
1112 W. Sixth, 320-8400, open weekdays until 10:30 and
weekends until midnight.

A lively late-night eatery is **Ruby's B.B.Q.**, behind
Antone's blues club at 2915 Guadalupe in the university
district, 477-1651, open nightly until 3:30 a.m.

Nightlife

Austin is the music capital of the Southwest. Bands based
here are the mainstay of a live music tour circuit that spans
from Little Rock to Colorado Springs to Santa Fe to Tucson.
If you haven't heard of Stevie Ray Vaughan, the Fabulous
Thunderbirds, and Charlie Sexton, maybe it's time you
introduced yourself to music Austin-style. Rock and R&B
have upstaged the country music scene in these parts, and
on a nighttime barhopping expedition along Sixth Street,
you'll find an eclectic musical smorgasbord including jazz,
rap, fusion, and reggae. Students make up much of the
audience, so cover charges are low, and it's simple and
affordable to wander into half a dozen or more clubs
within a few blocks of each other during the course of an
evening. Clubs in this district change frequently. Current
favorites include the **311 Club** (311 E. Sixth Street,
477-1630), **Babe's** (208 E. Sixth Street, 473-2262), **Carlin's**
(416 E. Sixth Street, 473-0905), and **Joe's Generic Bar**, 315
East Sixth Street, 480-0171. Austin's legendary blues venue
is **Antone's**, in the university district at 2915 Guadalupe,
474-5314.

The **Texas Tavern** in the University of Texas student
union is a concert and dance hall where local rock bands
on the rise perform nightly. The tavern is open to non-
students at a higher cover charge than students pay. A
quieter on-campus diversion is the Astronomy Department
Observatory atop Painter Hall on 24th Street, where the
telescope is open to the public for stargazing on Saturday
nights only, sunset to 10:30 p.m. when school is in session,

8:00 to 10:00 p.m. at other times. Admission is free. Also in the student union, the **Cactus Cafe and Bar** features name acts such as Leon Redbone and Townes Van Zandt in concert. For current concert information, call 471-8228.

LBJ COUNTRY

If this is your first visit to the Hill Country, it will dispel stereotypes about Texas once and for all. This green, rolling landscape dotted with small "Texas Dutch" villages is unlike any other part of Texas or, indeed, any other region on earth. Today you'll get a gentle introduction to the Hill Country from the perspective of its most famous resident, the late President Lyndon B. Johnson, as you visit historic sites that include his grandparents' homestead, his boyhood home, the "Texas White House," and his final resting place. You'll also have a chance to sample wild areas deep in the Hill Country.

Suggested Schedule	
9:00 a.m.	Leave Austin for the Hill Country.
10:00 a.m.	Visit Pedernales Falls State Park. Hike and picnic.
12:30 p.m.	Drive to Johnson City.
1:00 p.m.	Visit Johnson Settlement in the Johnson City Unit of Lyndon B. Johnson National Historical Park.
2:00 p.m.	Drive to LBJ Ranch.
2:30 p.m.	Visit Sauer-Beckmann Farmstead in Lyndon B. Johnson State Historical Park.
3:30 p.m.	Take the National Park Service bus tour of LBJ Ranch.
5:00 p.m.	Drive to Fredericksburg.
5:30 p.m.	Check into your accommodations. Go out to dinner and take an evening stroll around historic Fredericksburg.

Travel Route: Austin to Fredericksburg (65 miles)
Take US 290 west from Austin for 42 miles. It joins US 281; turn right (north) and go 6 miles to Johnson City.

Noncampers, who won't be returning to Pedernales Falls this evening, turn right (north) 34 miles out of Austin onto FR 3232 for 6 miles to the state park. Upon leaving the park, turn right (west) on the main road (which becomes FR 2766 at the curve near the park entrance) and drive 8 miles into Johnson City. At Johnson City, turn west on US 290 and drive 15 miles to the LBJ ranch.

Campers will return to Johnson City and take FR 2766 to Pedernales State Park, then retrace their route past LBJ Ranch to Fredericksburg tomorrow morning. Non-campers, upon leaving the LBJ Ranch, continue west on US 290 to Fredericksburg, 17 miles.

The Hill Country

The sparsely populated region in the center of Texas known as the Hill Country, spanning roughly 125 miles east to west and 75 miles north to south (about the same size as the state of Vermont), is a gentle-looking land covered by low live oak forests and meadows that burst forth with unparalleled displays of wildflowers each spring. Its idyllic appearance is somewhat deceiving. Labyrinthine canyons walled by sheer limestone cliffs made the Hill Country difficult for pioneers to penetrate. It was equally difficult to farm, for the land is semiarid, and when the rain does come, it brings flash floods. These harsh realities have kept a lot of the Hill Country free from development, looking much as it did in past centuries. The beauty of the landscape is subtle but ultimately enchanting.

The Hill Country was settled in the 1840s and 1850s by German immigrants. While many Germans were quick to adapt to Texas ways, they became alienated from Anglo settlers during the U.S. Civil War, when their antislavery sentiments brought them under suspicion and, in some cases, led to massacres of Germans by Confederate patriots. These incidents, combined with the region's isolation (most railroad lines avoided the rugged terrain of the Hill Country, and some settlements here were among the last places in the nation to get electricity), have meant that the so-called Texas Dutch people of the Hill Country have retained much of their unique culture, a blend of Old World and frontier traditions still evident in the many small, seemingly time-passed villages, each with its slender-spired, postcard-perfect little Lutheran church and

The Hill Country

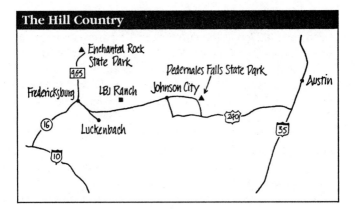

adjoining cemetery where rows and columns of grave-
stones stand regimented with Germanic precision. In family-
run restaurants and small general stores, you'll still hear the
guttural Texas Dutch drawl, perhaps the most unusual
regional accent in the English language.

Today, the Hill Country's distinctive character may be
eroding a little. Ever since Lyndon Johnson's presidency
exposed this hidden corner of America to network television cameras, ranches in the Hill Country have become
highly prized status symbols coveted by wealthy investors
from Houston and Dallas. A few towns have sprouted
clusters of condominiums and resort developments. And as
improved roads have put every part of the Hill Country
within a couple of hours' drive of Austin, San Antonio, or
Interstate 10, more and more young people have been
abandoning the region's slow, peaceful villages for the
bright lights just over the eastern horizon. Yet tradition is
strong here, and change happens slowly.

The day-and-a-half Hill Country segment of this itinerary
is designed only to provide first-time visitors with a tanta-
lizing taste of the region's charms. You may feel a yearning
to return next year and explore some more, to turn off the
"main" back roads on this route and find yourself on an
amazing lacework of ranch roads that take you ever
deeper into unknown territory. If you do, you'll discover
that it's easy to get lost back there. But then, I can't think
of a more delightful place to be lost.

Sightseeing Highlights

▲▲▲**Pedernales Falls State Park**—This 4,800-acre park preserves a wild landscape along several miles of the winding Pedernales River. (It's pronounced "purd-NAL-us," a perfect example of the traditional Texan tendency to mispronounce Spanish words whenever possible.) The falls themselves, reached by a ¼-mile trail descent from the end of the park road, are not what you'd normally think of as waterfalls, but they are beautiful. The river races down a sloping limestone slickrock staircase, pausing in a series of pretty, crystalline pools teeming with tiny fish, dropping just 50 feet in a distance of 3,000 feet. Bathing is prohibited at the falls, but there is a swimming area farther downriver on a different road, as well as a lovely picnic area. Hawks and vultures patrol the skies above the park, and deer are abundant, including exotic species originally imported from Europe and Asia as game animals but now protected year-round within the park boundaries. Hiking trails through the southern part of the park afford access to Hill Country wilderness for walks of half a day or more.

Campers who plan to spend the night in the park may wish to stop there briefly en route to Johnson City and the LBJ Ranch to reserve a campsite, especially during the summer months or on Fridays or Saturdays at any time of year, then return later in the day to enjoy the scenery. The park is open daily from 8:00 a.m. to 10:00 p.m. Admission is $2 per vehicle.

▲**Johnson City**—This crossroads town, now mainly a motel, restaurant, and gas station center catering to the many travelers who visit the LBJ Ranch, was named after Lyndon Johnson's grandfather, Sam Ealy Johnson, who established a ranch here and drove his longhorn cattle up the Chisholm Trail between 1867 and 1872. The ranch, known as Johnson Settlement, is now a unit of the Lyndon Johnson Historical Park. Leave your vehicle at the visitor center across the street from Lyndon Johnson's boyhood home, one block south of the main highway on G Street, and walk one block east on 9th Street, across Nugent Avenue, to the settlement entrance. A walking trail or an unpaved wagon road will lead you to the exhibit center, the original log cabin homestead, and other buildings that re-create ranch life in the late nineteenth century. The visitor center, boyhood home, and Johnson Settlement are open from 8:00 a.m. to 5:00 p.m. daily. Admission is free.

▲▲▲**LBJ Ranch**—To visitors who remember Lyndon Johnson's presidential administration, when the "Texas White House" was often in the public eye as the site of lavish barbecues for visiting foreign dignitaries and swarms of reporters and TV camera crews, and who imagined the ranch to approach the vast size of the King Ranch (Day 8), the most remarkable fact about the LBJ Ranch may be how small it actually is. A little over 2,000 acres, it is about the same size as a typical Texas State Park and capable of grazing about two dozen head of cattle. Yet the beauty of its setting explains Johnson's lifelong love for the Hill Country.

The back acreage of the ranch remains the private property of the Johnson family, while the front portion between the Pedernales River and the highway was given to the Texas State Parks and Wildlife Department. Two hundred acres, including the ranch house itself, have been deeded to the National Park Service and reserved as a life estate for Lady Bird Johnson, who lives there much of the time despite the tour buses cruising past her windows.

Start at the visitor center tour desk, where you will be given a colored token for one of the free 90-minute ranch tours that run at frequent intervals from 10:00 a.m. to 4:00 p.m. (5:00 p.m. during the summer months). The visitor center also contains, in addition to still more LBJ memorabilia, exhibits on the Hill Country and its people, past and present.

After boarding the tandem tour bus that takes you across the river to the main part of the ranch, your first brief stop will be at the one-room schoolhouse that Johnson attended for a year at age four in 1912. Fifty-three years later, as president, he chose this site to sign the Elementary and Secondary Education Act into law—with his old school-marm, Miss Kate Deadrich, acting as witness. There is a second, longer stop at a reconstruction of the four-room house where Lyndon Johnson was born. Though the original house, which had been a Johnson family home for 24 years, fell into disrepair after they moved back to Johnson City and was finally torn down in 1935, after acquiring the ranch Lyndon Johnson had this home rebuilt exactly like the original and furnished it with family possessions. During his presidency, it was used as lodging for favored members of the press corps. A short walk from the house is the peaceful little cemetery where Lyndon Johnson and other family members lie in the shade of a thousand-year-old oak tree. His is the biggest headstone.

Finally, the tour bus clears a Secret Service checkpoint and takes you for a spin around the exterior of the stately ranchhouse, then behind it for a look at airplane hangars, helicopter pads, and the working ranch areas. Since the National Park Service employs local people as guides, your driver will most likely speak with a "Texas Dutch" accent. There is an irony in this, since the Johnsons were practically the only non-German family in these parts. The "Texas Dutch" people being staunchly Republican, Lyndon Johnson never carried his home county in an election for the first twenty years of his political career.

Either before or after the ranch tour, be sure to visit Lyndon B. Johnson State Historical Park, which adjoins the visitor center. The centerpiece of the state park is the Sauer-Beckmann Farmstead, a German farm typical of the Hill Country, dating back to 1865 with a one-room log cabin, a cut-and-dressed limestone house, and a Victorian house. The state operates the farmstead as a working historic farm, and you may have a chance to see the staff planting, harvesting, canning, butchering, or making sausages in the smokehouse.

The state park also includes a half-mile nature trail that takes you past enclosures containing bison, javelinas, and wild turkeys as well as steers from the Texas State Longhorn Herd, probably your best opportunity for a closeup look at these magnificent animals. Unique to Texas, longhorn cattle descended from Spanish cattle that went wild during the 1700s. They evolved horns of exceptional length through "survival of the fittest," as a defense against prairie wolves. Although most nineteenth-century settlers got their start in ranching by rounding up wild longhorns, the cattle had practically vanished by the mid-twentieth century when the state of Texas began collecting its own herd to preserve them. Today, besides the state herd, ranchers in all parts of Texas breed longhorns as show animals.

The state park is open from 8:00 a.m. to 5:00 p.m. (6:00 p.m. in the summer months), with the farmstead closing half an hour earlier than the park. Admission to both national and state historical parks is free.

▲**Luckenbach**—For a scenic detour and an extra dose of Hill Country history along the way from LBJ Ranch to Fredericksburg, watch for Farm Road 1376 on your left. A 4-mile drive down this road will bring you to Luckenbach (pop. 25), a tiny hamlet that is something of a Texas legend. Back in the 1970s, a notorious local character by the name of Hondo Crouch bought the place and started inviting his friends down for lazy days of pickin' and grinnin' and beer and suchlike—folks like Willie Nelson, Waylon Jennings, and David Allen Coe. Luckenbach became the spiritual home of "Texas outlaw" music, which has become a country-western mainstay from Austin to Nashville. Today, it's usually a pretty uneventful place, though impromptu music and other interesting events sometimes happen around the general store on a Sunday afternoon.

The adventuresome might consider a road that turns off to your left as you retrace your route about halfway back to the main highway and eventually leads you into Fredericksburg by the back way. It goes past all that remains of Cain City, namely, a few small houses, one of which has flower boxes in front made of bricks from the old bank vault. Gone are the bank, hotel, warehouses, stores, post office, school, and lumberyard. You'd never know that back around 1915 this was one of the most important towns in the region. A short-lived railroad ran from here to San Antonio, making Cain City a shipping terminal for area farmers, including turkey growers who used to herd their fowl here all the way from Johnson City in flocks of a thousand or more. Yippy-ki-yi-yo, git along, little turkeys!

▲▲**Fredericksburg**—With a population of about 7,000, Fredericksburg is the most traditionally German of the Hill Country's major towns. On a stroll around town you'll see restored stone homes built in the 1850s by early settlers and motel room-sized "Sunday houses" used by distant ranch families when they came into town for church. The town's architectural showpiece is the Admiral Nimitz House. A detailed self-guided tour brochure covering the Fredericksburg historic district is available at the Chamber of Commerce, 112 W. Main Street.

Admiral Nimitz State Historical Park is downtown at 340 E. Main Street. Nimitz was the commander in chief of the Pacific in World War II, beginning 18 days after the attack at Pearl Harbor and continuing through the Japanese surrender four years later. He commanded more man-power and firepower than all military leaders in previous wars combined. Admiral Nimitz was born and raised in Fredericksburg, and like LBJ, his Hill Country roots go way back. The Nimitz historical park, though it focuses on America's war against Japan fifty years ago, is not just for military history buffs. The main building is in the old Nimitz Hotel, built by Admiral Nimitz's grandfather, Captain Charles Nimitz, a former German merchant marine ship's captain and one of Fredericksburg's first settlers. The old hotel incorporated nautical architecture, with a bridge and superstructure that may help explain what inspired a boy from the dry, landlocked Hill Country to become a great naval leader. Its guests have included Robert E. Lee, Ulysses S. Grant, and Jesse James. The old hotel is now the Museum of the Pacific War. At the back of the property is a picture-perfect Japanese garden, the Garden of Peace, a gift from the people of Japan. It is modeled after the gar-den of Japanese admiral Heihachiro Togo and includes a replica of Togo's study. A block north of the Japanese garden is a Pacific History Walk, a peaceful park strewn with war machinery. Environmentalists are working at establishing a nature walk along Town Creek between the

Japanese garden and the history walk. Admiral Nimitz State Historical Park is open daily from 8:00 a.m. to 5:00 p.m. Admission is $3 for adults, $1 for students and 50 cents for children ages 7 to 12.

The Pioneer Museum complex at 309 W. Main Street consists of a nine-room pioneer home and store dating back to 1850, as well as several smaller buildings including a Sunday house, all with period furnishings and artifacts. The museum is open daily except Tuesday from April through October, weekends only the rest of the year, from 10:00 a.m. (1:00 p.m. on Sundays) to 5:00 p.m. Admission is $2 for adults, 50 cents for students.

Lodging

Fredericksburg has about a dozen motels, easy to find, all within walking distance of downtown, ranging in price from about $35 to $50 per night double; but the motels here are actually outnumbered by bed and breakfasts. The B&Bs are typically small and traditional, run by Texans of German ancestry, with room rates for two ranging from about $40 to $60. Good possibilities include the **Fredericksburg Inn on the Square**, 102 W. Austin, (512) 997-3656; **The Delforge Place**, 710 Ettie Street, (512) 997-6212; the **Barons Creek Inn**, 110 E. Creek, (512) 997-9398; and the **J-Bar-K Ranch Bed & Breakfast**, a beautiful 1879 German-style rock home outside of town at Box 53A, (512) 669-2471. These and other bed and breakfast accommodations and homestays can be arranged through **Bed and Breakfast of Fredericksburg**, 405 E. Main Street, Fredericksburg, TX 78624, (512) 997-4712; **Gasthaus Schmidt**, 501 W. Main, Fredericksburg, TX 78624, (512) 997-5612; or **Bed & Breakfast Texas Style** (see Day 2).

Camping

Probably the most pleasant public campground in the Hill Country is at **Pedernales Falls State Park** (see Sightseeing Highlights above) near Johnson City. There are 69 spacious campsites with water and electric hookups. A nature trail takes you part way down limestone cliffs along a wild canyon, and many deer wander through the campground. Sites cost $9 per night.

Convenient to Fredericksburg is **Lady Bird Johnson Municipal Park**, 3 miles south of town on TX 16. This is a quite civilized little park with a golf course, a swimming pool, lighted tennis courts, a recreation room and children's playground, and a small lake for pedal-boating. Full-hookup sites cost $10 per night.

Primitive campsites (no hookups) are also available at **Enchanted Rock State Park** (see Sightseeing Highlights, Day 14), 18 miles north of Fredericksburg via Farm Road 965. Sites cost $6. Spending the night here would give you a chance to view sunset or sunrise from a magnificent vantage point on top of the rock. (You can't camp on top, though.)

Food

Texas barbecue is different in the Hill Country than elsewhere. Try the barbecued German-style sausage and thin-sliced beef brisket in sweet sauce at the little restaurant in Johnson City which has a sign out front advertising the "World's Best Chicken Fried Steak—Dozens and Dozens Sold."

For dinner in Fredericksburg, try **Friedhelm's Bavarian Inn** at 905 W. Main, 997-7024, closed Mondays. A good place for breakfast is **George's Old German Bakery & Restaurant**, which opens at 7:00 a.m., closed Tuesdays and Wednesdays.

The farms between Johnson City and Fredericksburg grow a lot of peaches, for sale at roadside stands during harvest season. If you see them, stock up.

MORE OF THE HILL COUNTRY

Today you'll have a chance to explore wild areas of the Hill Country before plunging into the Chihuahuan Desert to visit a full-sized re-creation of the Alamo built as a motion picture location, and then returning to the Rio Grande at Del Rio.

Suggested Schedule

9:00 a.m.	Drive to Enchanted Rock State Park.
9:30 a.m.	Climb Enchanted Rock.
10:30 a.m.	Return to Fredericksburg and drive to Lost Maples State Natural Area.
12:00 noon	Picnic and hike at Lost Maples.
3:00 p.m.	Drive to Del Rio.
5:00 p.m.	Arrive in Del Rio. Eat dinner and check into a motel or continue west out of town to a campground.

Travel Route: Fredericksburg to Del Rio (205 miles)
To drive from Fredericksburg to Enchanted Rock State Park, take Farm Road 965 due north from town for 18 miles. After about 13 miles, you will pass Crabapple Community, a ghost town with one of the finest groups of turn-of-the-century limestone buildings in the Hill Country, including a Lutheran church and a one-room schoolhouse. You are free to wander around the exteriors. After visiting Enchanted Rock, retrace your route back to Fredericksburg.

From Fredericksburg, go south on TX 16 for 24 miles to Kerrville, which is just south of I-10. Turn west on TX 27 for 8 miles to Ingram, then fork left on TX 39 through Hunt. About 26 miles from Ingram, watch on your left for Farm Road 187, which goes south to Lost Maples State Natural Area (17 miles).

Upon leaving Lost Maples, continue south on Farm Road 187 for 11 miles, past the little village of Vanderpool to Utopia. Turn right (west) on Farm Road 337 and drive 15 miles to Garner State Park, where you'll join US 83. Turn

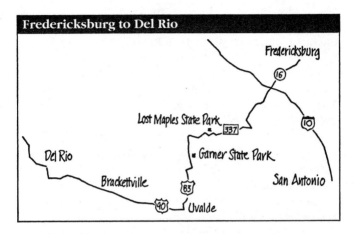

Fredericksburg to Del Rio

right on US 83 and drive south 32 miles to Uvalde. Turn
west on US 90. Brackettville, site of the Alamo movie set (7
miles north of the main highway on Farm Road 674), is 40
miles west across the desert. From there, another 32 miles
on US 90 will bring you to Del Rio.

Sightseeing Highlights

▲▲**Enchanted Rock State Park**—A Hill Country landmark and a tourist attraction as early as the 1850s, this
500-foot-high granite dome affords an incomparable,
panoramic view. To see for yourself, climb the 1-mile trail
to the summit. Near the top, on the north slope, is the
entrance to Enchanted Rock Cave, 1,000 feet deep and one
of the largest known granite caves. The rock derives its
name from legends of the Comanche Indians, who
believed that spirits lived here. The Indians are said to
have used the rock for human sacrifices, and ghostly lights
on the summit and strange noises are still reported sometimes. The park is open daily from 8:00 a.m. to 10:00 p.m.
Admission is $2 per vehicle.

▲▲**Lost Maples State Natural Area**—Groves of bigtooth
maples, which require precise growing conditions and
occur only in rare pockets throughout the Southwest,
provided the reason to set this wilderness area aside in its
natural state and gave the park its name. The park is
crowded during fall colors (November) but not at other

times. Twelve miles of backcountry loop trails from the trailhead at the end of the park road offer some of the finest hiking opportunities in the Hill Country. Wildlife includes abundant white-tailed deer and armadillos. Mountain lions also live in the park but are seldom seen. The day-use fee is $2 per vehicle.

▲**Garner State Recreation Park**—This 1,420-acre scenic area on the Frio River is more developed than other Hill Country parks, with cabins, a store, and a snack bar. You can swim, fish, hike, cruise around in a pedal-boat, or play miniature golf. The day-use fee is $2 per vehicle.

▲**Alamo Village Movie Location**—John Wayne went broke financing the lavishly produced 1959 film *The Alamo*. This is the movie set he spent his life savings on. It looks more like the Alamo of legend than the real Alamo does today in the shadows of San Antonio skyscrapers. There is also a full-sized, authentic West Texas frontier town used as a set for other movies. During the summer months you can ride a stagecoach and witness a shootout. Alamo Village is open daily from 9:00 a.m. until about sundown. Admission is $6 per adult, $3 for children ages 6 to 11; $1 per person discount off-season.

Lodging
Many, many motels line the US 90 strip for miles northwest of downtown Del Rio. Room rates range from about $30—sometimes less outside of the summer season—at budget-basic ma-and-pa motels like the **Remington Inn** (3808 Highway 90 West, 210-775-0585) to a high of $60 to $70 at the relatively luxurious **Ramada Inn** (2101 Avenue F, 210-775-1511). Shop and compare; you will not need advance reservations.

Camping
Seminole Canyon State Park (see Day 16 Sightseeing Highlights), about 40 miles west of Del Rio off US 90, has a campground on a desert hilltop. Sites cost $9 per night, with an extra $2 charge for electric hookup. Because of the distance out of town, those arriving in the Del Rio area late in the day may wish to settle for a Corps of Engineers or

privately owned campground near Amistad Lake on their
first night in the area and move here for their second night.
Camping at Seminole Canyon is convenient for those who
wish to take the morning ranger-guided hike into the
canyon.

There are seven Corps of Engineers camping areas near
the lakeshore on the United States side of **Amistad Lake**,
marked by signs along US 90 west of Del Rio and US 277
north of town. Intended mainly as a convenience for
boaters and fishermen, most of these campgrounds are
right next to the highway and can be noisy. The good
news is that they're free. Especially if you are arriving at
the lake around dusk or later, proceed with caution on any
road off the main highways; many of these roads pre-date
the lake, and they may suddenly disappear into the water
without much warning.

Food

Del Rio has about thirty restaurants, virtually all of them
located along US 90 (Avenue F). Try the **Cripple Creek
Saloon**, a family restaurant serving steaks and seafood 4
miles west of town on US 90, open Monday through Friday
from 5:00 to 10:00 p.m., Saturday 5:00 to 11:00 p.m., closed
Sundays (775-0153).

Generally, the best restaurants in the Del Rio area are
across the river in Ciudad Acuña, Mexico. See tomorrow's
Sightseeing Highlights for suggestions.

DEL RIO AND CIUDAD ACUÑA

In former days, Del Rio (pop. 31,000) was a sleepy border
town best known as the home of a radio station that
broadcast from a tower across the border, beyond FCC
jurisdiction, with such power that its country music and
evangelism could be heard across half the United States. In
1969, things changed with the completion of Amistad Dam,
which turned the confluence of the Rio Grande and the
Pecos River into a major destination for boating enthusiasts.
Del Rio is on the edge of nowhere. The nearest larger city
is San Antonio, 150 miles away, and following this itinerary
you won't come to another town the size of Del Rio for
nearly a week. Make this a lazy transition day as you
accustom yourself to the vast emptiness of West Texas.
The choice of pleasures is yours. Rent a boat and enjoy the
lake, explore the history of downtown Del Rio, or cross
the border into Ciudad Acuña, Mexico.

Suggested Schedule	
Morning	Take a walking tour of historic downtown Del Rio.
Afternoon	Cross the international bridge and wander through Ciudad Acuña.
Or	Forget about schedules, rent a boat, and spend the day on the water at Amistad Reservoir.

Getting Around the Del Rio Area
US 90 enters the city from the east as Gibbs Street but
takes a right turn on Avenue F downtown, taking you to
Courthouse Square. Turn left instead to reach the
Whitehead Memorial Museum (south on Main Street) and
the international bridge to Ciudad Acuña. Following
Avenue F north, you'll find yourself on westbound US 90,
a long strip of motels, chain restaurants, supermarkets, and
minimalls. Out past the end of town, a road branches
south to the international port of entry across Amistad

Del Rio Area

Dam. You can drive across the dam to Playa Tlaloc (Tlaloc Beach), marked by a big stone statue of its rain god namesake, and swim in Mexican waters. Continuing west on US 90, on your right just before the bridge over the lake are turnoffs to the Diablo Beach Marina and a swimming beach near the highway.

Sightseeing Highlights
▲▲**Del Rio**—This town dates back to the 1860s, when a rancher from Uvalde, searching for cattle driven off by the local Kickapoo Indians, discovered a desert spring and started a ranch at the oasis. The railroad came to Del Rio in the 1880s, bringing prosperity and Italian immigrants who established vineyards and a winery, the only one in Texas until recently, and who possessed the stonecutting skills to build the fine historic structures you can see today in the Courthouse Square area. The county courthouse itself, built in 1887 of local limestone, is one of the most

fanciful in Texas, a touch of Old World elegance on the far
reaches of the American frontier. A walking tour of the
Courthouse Square area is available from the chamber of
commerce at 1915 Avenue F.

The Whitehead Memorial Museum at 1308 S. Main Street
has a collection of original and replica nineteenth-century
buildings that re-create the feel of Del Rio's days as a
frontier boomtown. Judge Roy Bean is buried here beside
a copy of his saloon. (For the real thing, see tomorrow's
Sightseeing Highlights.) The Whitehead Memorial Museum
is open Tuesday through Saturday from 9:00 a.m. to 4:30
p.m., closed Sundays and Mondays. Admission is $2 for
adults, 50 cents for students ages 6 to 18.

▲▲**Amistad National Recreation Area**—This reservoir
fed by the Rio Grande and the Pecos River is the third-
largest manmade lake in the United States and the largest
body of water on the U.S./Mexican border. Six-mile-long
Amistad Dam impounds a reservoir 85 miles long, flooding
a labyrinth of desert canyons. Most of the shoreline is
inaccessible by road. Absolute solitude is easy to find on
weekdays. This could be the day to take a break from
driving and rent a boat. National Recreation Area conces-
sionaires rent boats at Diablo East Marina, 774-2003, on US
90 and Rough Canyon Marina, 775-8779, on Recreation
Road 2 off US 277 north of Del Rio. Private boat rentals are
available from Oasis Boat & Ski Rental, 775-9695, at the
American Campground near Del Rio. Powerboats rent for
$90 to $150 per day, while Sunfish sailboats rent for about
$40 a day.

▲▲**Ciudad Acuña**—This small city across the Rio Grande
from Del Rio feels more completely Mexican than other
south-of-the-border cities on the itinerary route. The attractions of Ciudad Acuña are similar to those of Matamoros or
Ciudad Juárez: produce and handicrafts markets, souvenir
shops, restaurants, nightclubs, and bullfights, but the scale
is smaller because Ciudad Acuña is off the beaten path. As
soon as you cross the pedestrian bridge south of Del Rio
and emerge in downtown Ciudad Acuña, you'll feel like
you're in a foreign place. Wander deep and browse.

Ciudad Acuña's economy depends primarily on tourism, and several of the restaurants there serve better food at lower prices in a more comfortable atmosphere than their highwayside counterparts north of the river. For example, try **Lando's Restaurant** at Hidalgo 270 Oeste, **Manuel's Restaurant** at Hidalgo 239 Oeste, **Fiesta Gallas** at Hidalgo 320, or **Crosby's** at the corner of Hidalgo and Matamoros.

See "How to Use This Book" for information on crossing the border.

DRIVING TO BIG BEND

At first, taking a trip through West Texas can feel like vacationing on the moon. Across the dry, gouged, barren landscape, home to spiny flora and poisonous fauna, you see nobody. All the countryside for hundreds of miles between Amistad Reservoir and Big Bend is privately owned ranchland—look but don't touch. Trespassing laws are strict out here, though even cattle need many square miles to graze, so you'll rarely see either cowboy or steer.

The Chihuahuan Desert experience unfolds slowly as, along miles of open, empty road, you notice the strange elegance of the plants—lechuguilla, ocotillo, resurrection plant, oregano, purple sage, century plant—that survive in this harsh land, and you see cave paintings created by people who lived out here before Jesus was born, Rome was founded, or the first Egyptian pyramid was built. Since then, the population of West Texas hasn't grown very much. Therein lies its charm.

Suggested Schedule	
9:00 a.m.	Leaving Del Rio, drive to Seminole Canyon State Park.
10:00 a.m.	Tour the painted caves in Seminole Canyon.
11:30 a.m.	Drive to Langtry.
12:00 noon	Stop in at the Judge Roy Bean Visitors Center.
12:30 p.m.	Picnic.
1:00 p.m.	Drive to Big Bend National Park.
4:00 p.m.	Arrive in Big Bend National Park. Stop in at the Panther Junction Visitors Center.
5:00 p.m.	Arrive at Chisos Basin in the center of the park. Camp or check into the lodge for two nights.

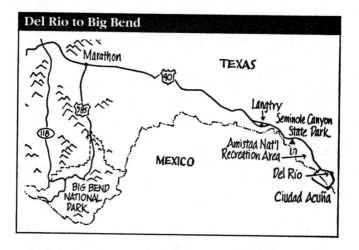

Del Rio to Big Bend

Travel Route: Del Rio to Chisos Basin, Big Bend National Park (253 miles)

Stock up on groceries before leaving Del Rio. You won't see another supermarket or much in the way of restaurants until you reach El Paso on the evening of Day 20. When traveling in West Texas, fill up on gasoline at every opportunity and always carry plenty of water just in case.

Take US 90 west toward Marathon. Seminole Canyon State Park is about 30 miles west of Del Rio off US 90, and Langtry is another 25 miles west. From Langtry, Marathon is another 120 empty miles to the west. At Marathon, take US 385 south for 40 miles to the national park boundary and continue for 39 more miles to the national park village at Chisos Basin.

Sightseeing Highlights

▲▲**Seminole Canyon State Park**—Seminole Canyon contains caves that were occupied by hunting-and-gathering Indians for thousands of years. The Indians painted pictographs on the back walls and ceilings of the caves using natural earth pigments. Layer upon layer of paintings cover the whole 500-foot length of the largest cave, depicting shamans, game animals, strange figures like space men and giant insects, and many symbols whose meanings remain a mystery. The oldest paintings date back to about

6000 B.C.—the earliest surviving artwork in North America. The visitors center has reproductions of some of the paintings, but the only way you can enter the canyon and see the real paintings in the caves is on a one-hour ranger-guided hike into the canyon. Tours leave from the visitors center Wednesday through Sunday at 10:00 a.m. and 3:00 p.m. The visitors center is open from 8:00 a.m. to 5:00 p.m. The park fee is $2 per vehicle.

▲▲**Judge Roy Bean Visitors Center**—Judge Roy Bean was a saloonkeeper, justice of the peace, and coroner in the small town of Langtry (present-day population 30, on a loop from the main highway about 60 miles west of Del Rio). After losing an election, he bought the office of jus- tice of the peace from his opponent for a demijohn of whiskey, two bearskins, and a pet raccoon and held the position unchallenged for more than thirty years to become one of West Texas's best-known colorful charac- ters, the self-styled "Law West of the Pecos." Eccentric and none too law-abiding himself, Bean ignored the Texas state statutes, preferring an antique copy of the laws of his home state of California published in 1856. He not only married people but also granted divorces, even though they were prohibited by Texas law, and he made sure that unlawful sporting events such as bullfights and shootouts took place across the Rio Grande, outside of his jurisdic- tion. Fascinated by Bean's creative approach to justice, magazine writers and dime novelists from the East made him nationally famous as a sort of jurisprudential Robin Hood of the Wild West. More recently, Bean was immortal- ized in a 1950s television series and a 1970s motion picture starring Paul Newman as the judge.

The Jersey Lilly Saloon, where Judge Bean held court, is now in the courtyard of the Texas State Visitor Center in Langtry, which also has a desert garden providing an introduction to the strange plant life of the Chihuahuan Desert. The visitor center is open daily from 8:00 a.m. to 5:00 p.m. Admission is free.

▲▲▲**Big Bend National Park**—This is the wildest corner of Texas. With an area of 1,100 square miles, the park spans over 100 miles of shoreline and canyon rim along

the Rio Grande and includes the Chisos Mountains with
summits of up to 7,835 feet, more than a mile above river
level. The entrance fee of $5 per vehicle is good for stays
of up to a week.

Wildlife is abundant along the river and in the mountains.
Watch for javelinas (small wild pigs also known as collared
peccaries) as well as deer, desert bighorn sheep, and
eagles. Mountain lions, coyotes, and bears also live in
the park.

Arriving at Big Bend this afternoon, stop at the visitor
center at Panther Junction, where US 385 meets the main
park road. Visitors planning to camp at the Basin or spend
the night in Chisos Mountain Lodge should proceed west
on the park road for 5 miles to the Basin road, which
winds up over Panther Pass and into the bowl-shaped
center of the Chisos Mountains. The Spanish name Chisos
means "ghosts." Set up camp and relax. Tomorrow will be
soon enough to explore the rest of the park. From the
Basin Trailhead, the short Window View Trail is an ideal
half-hour sunset walk. A longer hike from the Basin is the
4-mile trail up to The Window for a panoramic view of
rugged mountains to the west.

Lodging and Food
The **Chisos Mountains Lodge** at Chisos Basin in Big
Bend National Park has only 34 guest rooms, so advance
reservations are in order. Call (915) 477-2352 or write
Chisos Mountains Lodge, Basin Rural Station, Big Bend
National Park, TX 79834-9999. Double rooms run $53 to
$70. The lodge dining room serves three meals a day.

Outside the park, 69 miles away in Marathon (at the
junction of US 90 and US 385, before you reach Big Bend
following the travel route described above) is the **Gage
Hotel**, built in 1928 by a San Antonio banker who
acquired a large ranch in the Big Bend region but found
that there was no place to stay while visiting his spread.
The 20-room brick hotel has recently been restored, and
while its accommodations would hardly be considered
luxurious by big-city standards, it offers a genuine feel of
West Texas in an earlier era. Rooms start around $35. For

reservations, call (915) 386-4205. The hotel's restaurant is open daily from 6:30 a.m. to 2:30 p.m. and 6:00 to 9:30 p.m.

Camping

There are three national park service campgrounds as well as a small private concession RV park in Big Bend National Park. The most spectacular setting is that of **Basin Campground**, in the central bowl of the rugged Chisos Mountains, near the Chisos Mountains Lodge with its restaurant. Because of the steep, winding road into the Basin, trailers over 20 feet and RVs over 24 feet in length are discouraged here.

Rio Grande Village Campground, near the bank of the Rio Grande about 20 miles southeast of Panther Junction, has nature trails and a laundromat but no restaurant. At a lower elevation, Rio Grande Village is warmer than Basin Campground during the winter months. It is popular with "winter Texans" and fishermen, and with 200 sites it is much larger than Basin Campground.

Camping at either Basin or Rio Grande Village costs $5 in addition to the park admission. There are no hookups. The Rio Grande Village Camp Store rents 25 campsites with electric, water, and sewer hookups on a first-come, first-served basis; prices for these are substantially higher than the park service campgrounds.

Cottonwood Campground is also on the river, in the southwest part of the park at Castolon near Santa Elena Canyon. Its more remote location and proximity to the remains of a historic village make it attractive; however, it is the most primitive of the three park service campgrounds, and the restrooms consist of pit toilets only, no running water or electricity. (Drinking water is available nearby.) The camping fee is $3 per night.

BIG BEND NATIONAL PARK

Big Bend is a large park, and most of the routes through it call for travel on horseback, by raft, or in a four-wheel-drive vehicle. All of these can be arranged through guide services in the vicinity. For free, you can reach three contrasting areas of the park—the Chisos Mountains, Rio Grande Village, and Santa Elena Canyon—by passenger car. The following plan covers every part of Big Bend National Park that can be reached by paved road and describes hiking possibilities in each area.

Suggested Schedule

8:00 a.m.	Hike a trail in the Chisos Mountains, such as the one up Lost Mine Peak.
12:00 noon	Return to your vehicle. Drive to Rio Grande Village.
12:30 p.m.	At Rio Grande Village, follow the trail down to the river and a secluded picnic spot.
2:00 p.m.	Drive to Castolon and Santa Elena Canyon.
3:30 p.m.	Arrive at Castolon. Explore the old trading post.
4:00 p.m.	Take a short walk up Santa Elena Canyon.
5:00 p.m.	Return to the Chisos Mountains Lodge. (Campers may wish to stay at Castolon instead.)

Sightseeing Highlights
▲▲**Chisos High Country Hiking**—The Chisos Mountains are the most popular hiking area in Big Bend. The most beautiful trail in the park is also one of the most ambitious— the 13-mile round-trip South Rim Trail. It leads from the Basin Trailhead up into the surrounding mountains, where it intersects several other trails through the high Chisos, including one that goes to the top of Emory Peak, the highest mountain in the

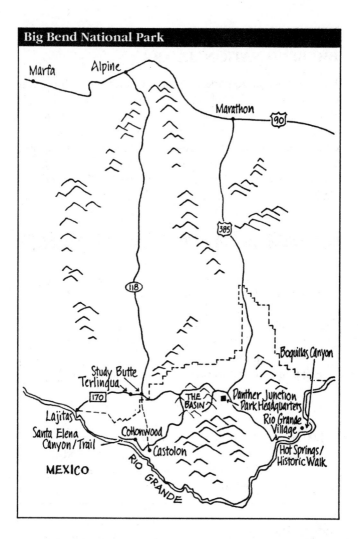

Big Bend National Park

Marfa · Alpine · Marathon · [90] · [385] · [118] · Study Butte · Terlingua · [170] · THE BASIN · Panther Junction Park Headquarters · Boquillas Canyon · Lajitas · Cottonwood · Rio Grande Village · Santa Elena Canyon/Trail · Castolon · Hot Springs/Historic Walk · MEXICO · RIO GRANDE

park. To hike the high country takes all day. Bring plenty of water.

For a half-day high country hike, drive back out the Basin road to the summit of Panther Pass and hike from there on the 5-mile round-trip Lost Mine Trail. Starting from the top of the pass saves your legs the climb out of the Basin, leaving only a 1,250-foot ascent to the summit of Lost Mine Peak, elevation 7,550 feet.

▲**Rio Grande Village and Boquillas Canyon**—From Basin Junction, turn right and take the main park road south for 23 miles to Rio Grande Village, where three short walks will show you various aspects of the river. The easy Rio Grande Village Nature Trail takes you through dense floodplain vegetation to a hilltop with a view of the river. The Hot Springs Trail, 2 miles round-trip, leads to the ruins of a 1909 homestead and hot springs resort; the 105-degree springs still feed the pool in the foundation of the old bathhouse. The 1-mile round-trip Boquillas Canyon Trail goes up over a limestone ridge and then down to the river. Allow an hour for either of the latter hikes.

▲▲**Castolon and Santa Elena Canyon**—This area is on the far side of the park, a 55-mile drive from Rio Grande Village. Retrace your route from there to Basin Junction, then drive 10 miles west to Santa Elena Junction. Turn south and follow the Ross Maxwell Scenic Drive for 22 miles to Castolon. This former U.S. Army fort became a border trading post in the early 1900s. Today you can take a self-guided walking tour of the historical compound. A gas station and grocery store operate in Castolon. Continue west on the scenic drive for another 8 miles to reach an overlook and view Santa Elena Canyon to the west. From the paved road's end at the river, the short Santa Elena Canyon Trail takes you upriver to a place where the Rio Grande is crowded close between 1,500-foot cliffs.

Instead of returning to the main park road the same way you came, you can make the Santa Elena Canyon into a loop trip by following the road north from the overlook. It is unpaved but passable by passenger vehicle without four-wheel drive. The route takes you past the ruins of an old Mexican village known as Terlingua Abaja and the homestead of early settler Gilberto Luna as it takes you 13 miles back to the paved park road at an intersection near the west park entrance, 23 miles west of Basin Junction.

Other Big Bend Activities—Most of Big Bend National Park is not accessible to low-clearance passenger cars; because of the large distances involved, much of it is not accessible to hikers either. Here are some other ways to explore:

Four-wheel-drive roads cross most parts of the park. If you have a Jeep or mountain bike, stop at the Panther Junction Visitor Center to pick up a map and check on current road conditions, then go and explore. Be sure you have plenty of water, a full tank of gas, a good spare tire, and a tire inflation can or tire repair kit. This is thorny country, and flat tires are a likelihood.

River rafting is growing in popularity as a way to see the Big Bend river canyons. For complete information on raft trips, contact Far Flung Adventures, P.O. Box 31, Terlingua, TX 79852, (915) 371-2489; Outback Expeditions, P.O. Box 44, Terlingua, TX 79852, (915) 371-2490; or Big Bend River Tours, Lajitas, TX 79852, (800) 545-4240.

Saddle horse rentals and guided horseback trips into the Chisos high country can be arranged through Chisos Remuda at the Basin. Call (915) 477-2374 for complete information and reservations.

▲▲**Big Bend Ranch State Natural Area**—This vast area along the Rio Grande west of Big Bend National Park is larger than all other units of the Texas State Parks system combined. Acquired by the state in 1989, Big Bend Ranch is still in the very early stages of development as a park. You can drive through it on paved TX 170, which runs from the national park's west entrance to enter the state natural area at Lajitas and follow the river for about 50 miles, much of it through the volcanic Bofecillos Mountains, to the quiet little village of Presidio, the self-proclaimed Onion Capital of the World, where a 19th-century private border fortress-trading post has been preserved as Fort Leaton State Historic Site. The Fort is open daily from 8:00 a.m. to 4:30 p.m. ($1 for adults, 50 cents for children under 12) and doubles as a visitors center for Big Bend Ranch. Along the highway are three trailheads into the backcountry of the ranch. Of these, the ¾-mile Closed Canyon Trail makes a good short sight-seeing hike. You can obtain a hiking permit, as well as information on longer trails that lead into the heart of the natural area, from the Fort Leaton visitors center in Presidio or the Barton Warnock Environmental Education Center in Lajitas. The park service runs bus tours through Big Bend

Ranch twice a month. One starts from Fort Leaton on the first Saturday of each month and the other from the Warnock Center on the third Saturday. Both depart at 8:00 a.m. and last all day. The tour is $30 per person, and reservations are essential. For current information and reservations, call Big Bend Ranch headquarters at (915) 424-3327.

EXPLORING WEST TEXAS

Take your time driving north from Big Bend to the other national park in West Texas, spending this afternoon and evening in the Davis Mountains, where you'll discover a preserved frontier cavalry fort set up to defend early pioneers from Indian attacks, a beautiful hiking area, and maybe even an unexplained phenomenon.

Suggested Schedule

9:00 a.m.	Leave Big Bend National Park.
12:00 noon	Arrive in Fort Davis. Lunch.
1:00 p.m.	Drive up Mount Locke to W. J. McDonald Observatory.
2:00 p.m.	Tour the observatory.
3:00 p.m.	Return to Fort Davis.
3:30 p.m.	Visit old Fort Davis.
4:30 p.m.	Visit Davis Mountains State Park. Take a hike. You may wish to spend the night there at the campground or Indian Lodge.
6:00 p.m.	Eat in the Indian Lodge dining room.
Later	Can you resist taking a cool night drive to watch for the mysterious Marfa Lights?

Travel Route: Chisos Basin to Fort Davis (132 miles)
In Big Bend National Park, drive the main park road to the west entrance, a distance of 28 miles from the lodge and campground at Chisos Basin. Then follow TX 118 north for 104 miles through Alpine (pop. 5,500) to Fort Davis (pop. 900).

Sightseeing Highlights
▲**W. J. McDonald Observatory**—The night sky in West Texas, high in the mountains and hundreds of miles from city lights, is as dark as any in the continental United States, making the summit of Mount Locke (elevation 6,802 feet) an ideal place from which to view the stars. In the daytime, this astronomy observatory commands a

panoramic view. In the visitor center, exhibits include a collection of meteorites and a simulation where you can roll marbles or coins into a "black hole."

To reach the observatory, drive north on TX 118 for 17 steep miles, then turn southeast at the sign and drive 2 more miles up the mountain. The center is open daily from 9:00 a.m. to 5:00 p.m. Tours are at 2:00 p.m. daily, with additional tours at 9:30 a.m. during the summer months. Admission is free. Stargazing parties are held at sunset on Tuesdays, Fridays, and Saturdays, and solar viewing sessions are conducted daily at 11:00 a.m. The 107-inch telescope is open to visitors (suggested donation $5 for adults, $2.50 for children) one night per month; since this is the only observatory in the nation that makes its largest telescope available for public viewing, you must make reservations about six months in advance. For more information, contact the McDonald Observatory Visitors' Information Center, Box 1337, Fort Davis, TX 79734, or call (915) 426-3640.

▲▲**Fort Davis National Historic Site**—This frontier cavalry fort was built in 1854, abandoned during the Civil War, and rebuilt in 1867 to guard the road between San Antonio and El Paso from Comanche Indian attacks. By the time the fort was deactivated in 1891, it consisted of seventy adobe and stone structures. Fort Davis is the best-preserved of seven cavalry forts of the pioneer era that remain standing in West Texas. The visitor center displays military and Indian artifacts from the time when Fort Davis was active. The fort is open daily from 8:00 a.m. to 5:00 p.m. (until 6:00 during the summer months). Admission is $1 per adult, children under 17 and senior citizens free.

▲**Chihuahuan Desert Research Center**—Stop in at the visitor center and walk through the 30-acre arboretum for insights into the ways the desert works. There are also nature trails throughout the 500-acre grounds of this private nonprofit research center just south of Fort Davis. The visitor center is only open from late April through Labor Day, Monday through Friday from 1:00 to 5:00 p.m., Saturday and Sunday 9:00 a.m. to 6:00 p.m. Admission is free.

▲▲**Davis Mountains State Park**—Soft, rolling mountains covered with grassy meadows and live oak, strikingly different from the jagged mountains in Big Bend, are the setting for this 1,800-acre park adjoining historic Indian Lodge (see Lodging below). Miles of trails make the park the best place in the Davis Mountains for hiking; the rest of the mountain range, beautiful to drive through, is private ranchland posted "no trespassing." To get to Davis Mountains State Park, take TX 118 past Fort Davis National Historic Site and turn on the clearly marked park road. It is open daily from 8:00 a.m. to 10:00 p.m. A nature center is open in the afternoons during the summer months only. Admission is $2 per vehicle.

▲**Marfa Lights**—To add a nighttime adventure to your trip and perhaps encounter a mystery worth telling the folks back home about, drive south after dark to the town of Marfa, 21 miles south of Fort Davis on TX 17. Marfa has two claims to fame. It was the location for the classic film *Giant*, starring the late Rock Hudson and the late James Dean, but the facades of Riata Ranch have long since vanished. To watch for the other Marfa attraction, turn east from town on US 67/90 and drive about 9 more miles to the Official Marfa Lights Viewing Site with its State Historical Marker. Here, many people see one of the world's best-documented cases of "ghost lights." Apaches who lived nearby in the late nineteenth century said that the lights manifested the spirit of a great deceased chief named Alsate, and some people who give credence to the legend point out that they do bear a striking resemblance to Carlos Castaneda's description of a similar phenomenon in his books about the Yaqui Indian sorcerer Don Juan. UFO buffs have different ideas, while scientists from McDonald Observatory who have studied the lights extensively can offer no explanation whatsoever. The lights have been reported regularly for over 100 years. They have been photographed and videotaped, but nobody has succeeded in approaching them. One, two, or more, they dance fairy-like through the hills within a few miles in either direction from the viewing area, and on any given night you're as likely to see them as not.

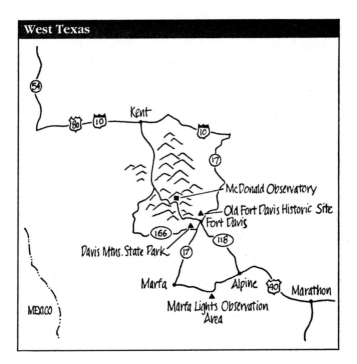

West Texas

Lodging

If you'd like to spend a night at a real, working Texas ranch, make reservations at the **Prude Ranch**, P.O. Box 1431, Fort Davis, TX 79734, (915) 426-3502. The ranch has been hosting visitors since 1911. A large indoor swimming pool, tennis courts, and horseback riding on miles of trails through live oak country in the Davis Mountains make this an attractive possibility for spending an extra day. Accommodations for two cost $75 per night. The cafeteria-style dining room serves home-grown meat entrées. There are also campsites with full RV hookups.

Indian Lodge in Davis Mountains State Park is a striking adobe complex built by the Civilian Conservation Corps in the 1930s. Rooms for two cost $45 to $55 per night, and meals in the lodge dining room are also surprisingly affordable. Guests can enjoy the park's hiking trails. For reservations, write Indian Lodge, P.O. Box 786, Fort Davis, TX 79734, or call (915) 426-3254. No pets; closed part of January.

In the town of Fort Davis (pop. 900) is the historic
Limpia Hotel, a restored 1912 inn with rustic oak
furniture, a veranda, and an enclosed sun porch. Rooms
cost $59 to $65. Call (915) 426-3237. Limpia means "clean"
in Spanish.

Camping
Davis Mountains State Park, 6 miles west of Fort Davis
off TX 118, has 88 campsites in a broad basin at an
elevation of 5,200 feet. Spend the early evening and early
morning hours discovering why this is one of the most
popular hiking and wildlife-watching areas in West Texas.
Campsites cost $8. A small number of sites with electric
hookups are available for $2 more.

DAVIS MOUNTAINS, GUADALUPE MOUNTAINS, AND CARLSBAD CAVERNS

The two national parks in the Guadalupe Mountains, separated only by a state line and about 13 miles of private ranchland, are like different aspects of a single park. Guadalupe Mountains National Park is a backcountry wilderness preserved for the pleasure of hikers; Carlsbad Caverns National Park contains a unique natural wonder visited by 800,000 people a year and the world's deepest subterranean lunchroom. Take time this afternoon and tomorrow morning to explore both parks.

Suggested Schedule

9:00 a.m.	Leave Fort Davis.
12:30 p.m.	Enter Guadalupe Mountains National Park. Stop at the visitors center, picnic, and spot a trail you may wish to hike on the return trip tomorrow morning.
2:00 p.m.	Arrive at Carlsbad Caverns National Park. Check into your accommodations or campsite at White's City.
3:00 p.m.	Take the Blue Tour (or the shorter Red Tour) into Carlsbad Caverns.
Sunset	In summer, stick around for the bat flight from the cave entrance.

Travel Route: Fort Davis to Carlsbad Caverns National Park (189 miles)

From Fort Davis, drive scenic TX 118 north through the Davis Mountains, a distance of 52 miles (it will seem twice that far) to Kent. Get on I-10 and drive 37 fast miles west to the next town, Van Horn. Exit north on TX 54 and drive 55 miles to the junction with US 62/180. At this intersection you enter the Mountain time zone and begin climbing the Guadalupe Mountains. It's 28 miles on US 62/180 to the Texas/New Mexico state line and 17 more miles to White's City and the entrance to Carlsbad Caverns National Park.

Sightseeing Highlights

▲▲**Guadalupe Mountains National Park**—If you only
see this park through a windshield, it appears as a steep
road that climbs up along the base of a sheer 2,000-foot
limestone cliff and leads eventually to Carlsbad Caverns.
To discover what is so special about Guadalupe Mountains
National Park, get out of your vehicle and walk, for this is
a park where the best parts are out of sight of the road, as
hidden as Carlsbad Cavern beneath the mountain. You'll
want to hurry past the turnoffs this afternoon to reach
Carlsbad Caverns National Park with plenty of time to take
the self-guided cave tour, but make a mental note of the
starting point for a Guadalupe Mountains hike to take
tomorrow morning.

Above the rim of the cliff are Guadalupe Peak (at 8,749
feet, the highest mountain in Texas) and an area called the
Bowl where Douglas fir and ponderosa pine tower, all that
remains of an ancient forest that covered most of West
Texas during the last Ice Age, when this area was home to
camels, mammoths, and Indians who hunted them. Today,
deer, elk, and even bears are common in the Bowl.
However, the high country is hard to reach, only accessible
by a steep, strenuous all-day hike starting from the Pinery,
the first picnic and camping area on your left as you climb
the highway.

A short distance up the main road from the Pinery, you'll
reach the park visitors center at Frijole Historic Site. There
you'll find historic ranch buildings and the easy Smith
Spring Trail, a 2-mile loop that takes you to two spring-fed
oases, Smith Spring and Manzanita Spring. Allow 1½ hours
for this hike, an ideal quick introduction to the Guadalupe
Mountains.

If you would like a longer hike, take the McKittrick
Canyon Trail up the creek among ponderosa pine, walnut,
maple, and madrone trees. The canyon is most spectacular
in its autumn colors. The trail starts from a trailhead near
McKittrick Canyon Visitor Center, at the end of a clearly
marked 3-mile side road on your left about 5 miles beyond
Frijole Visitor Center. It goes through the canyon for 4
miles, passing an old cabin built by geologist Walter Pratt,

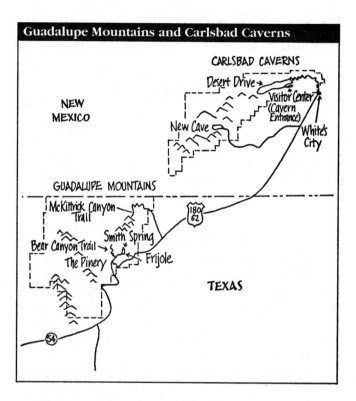

Guadalupe Mountains and Carlsbad Caverns

who later gave the federal government the first parcels of
land to create this national park, and finally reaching the
Grotto, with a spring, ferns and lush vegetation, and cave
formations. Allow four to six hours to hike the whole
distance up and back, or take just part of the trail for a
shorter walk.

Admission to Guadalupe Mountains National Park is free.
The visitor centers at Frijole and McKittrick Canyon are
open daily from 7:00 a.m. to 6:00 p.m. during the summer
months and 8:00 a.m. to 4:30 p.m. the rest of the year.
▲▲▲**Carlsbad Caverns National Park**—It's not exactly
in Texas, but now that you're out here in the vicinity, it
would be unthinkable to pass up a chance to visit Carlsbad
Caverns, the region's most popular national park, less than
20 miles north of the New Mexico state line.

Despite the park name, the cave most people visit is a

single cavern. Explorers have charted at least 21 miles of
Carlsbad Cavern, but only the first 3 miles are open to the
public, down as far as the Big Room, which is the largest
known subterranean chamber in the world. The Big Room
contains more space than the Houston Astrodome, and the
Texas State Capitol Building would fit in one end of it.

For the quickest possible look at Carlsbad Cavern, take
the Red Tour, by elevator both ways, descending directly
to the Big Room, 754 feet beneath the visitor center, for a
self-guided tour with optional interpretive commentary
from the personal radios for rent at the start of the trip. It
takes a while to appreciate this chamber's immensity since
you cannot see the whole room from a single vantage
point. Awe sets in slowly as you stroll the paved pathways
among monoliths and bottomless pits through this vast
natural cathedral sculptured in travertine and crystalized
calcite with fancifully named formations that the imagination may see as animals, draperies, kachinas, frozen waterfalls, demons, or erotic images. Allow at least 1½ hours for
the Red Tour. Lunch and curios are sold down in the
cavern near the elevator.

The longer Blue Tour, which takes about three hours,
lets you walk down to the Big Room from the natural cave
entrance near the visitor center, then ride the elevator back
up. Besides taking you through several smaller but exquis-
ite chambers that can't be seen on the shorter trip, the Blue
Tour lets you retrace the route of the cave's first explorer,
Jim White, and feel something of his surprise upon discovering the huge room at the bottom. White, a cowboy-
turned-bat-guano-digger who worked in the cave's natural
entrance, was more curious than his fellow miners who
had been shoveling here for more than a decade. He made
his way through the opening at the far end of the guano
pit and down into the darkness. Upon discovering what
was down there, White changed careers again and spent
the next twenty years guiding tours into Carlsbad Cavern
before it was declared a national monument in 1923. There
was no elevator in those days, and White lowered visitors
down into the cave entrance in guano buckets.

The cavern opens at 8:30 a.m. daily all year. You can start the self-guided Blue Tour from the natural cave entrance any time before 3:30 p.m. from Memorial Day to Labor Day, 2:00 p.m. the rest of the year. The shorter Red Tour, descending to the Big Room by elevator, continues running until 5:00 p.m. during the summer and 3:30 p.m. the rest of the year. Admission is $5 per adult and $3 per child ages 6 to 15. Radio receivers for the self-guided tour rent at 50 cents each.

Carlsbad Cavern is not the only cave in the park. The Slaughter River Cave is smaller but gives you a chance to experience what Carlsbad Cavern was like before elevators, paved walkways, tourist concessions, or electricity. The cave entrance is in the national park backcountry, reached by driving 11 miles west of the main highway from the turnoff 6 miles south of White's City. Visitors can only enter the cave on two-hour ranger-guided trips, which are conducted daily from Memorial Day to Labor Day, weekends only the rest of the year. Reservations are required, and you can make them up to two weeks in advance by calling the park at (505) 785-2232 or check at the visitor center about tomorrow's trips. The cost of the Slaughter River Cave trip is $6 for adults, $3 for children ages 6 to 15 (not recommended for younger children). Bring a flashlight.

Lechuguilla Cave, which was discovered in Carlsbad Caverns National Park in 1987, is longer and deeper than Carlsbad Cavern and has not yet been fully explored. Ever since the discovery, a controversy over what to do with the cave has been raging between local residents, who believe that paving and lighting a second cave would mean more tourist dollars for the depressed economy of Carlsbad, New Mexico, and conservationists, who want the pristine cave protected from development under the federal Wilderness Preservation Act as the nation's first official underground wilderness area. In the meantime, Lechuguilla Cave is only open to experienced spelunkers under permits with tight restrictions, but you can see photographs of its interior in the Carlsbad Caverns Visitor Center.

Lodging, Camping, and Food
Named for Jim White, the cowboy who discovered
Carlsbad Caverns in the 1880s, White's City is a cluster of
concessions at the entrance to the national park. Here
you'll find the **Best Western Caverns Inn**, with rooms for
two at $60 to $80 per night from mid-May through Labor
Day and as low as $50 the rest of the year, as well as
restaurants, a grocery store/gift shop/laundromat/museum,
and an RV park with hookups for $15 per night. Call (505)
785-2291 or, for reservations toll-free, (800) CAVERNS.

More affordable accommodations can be found 13 miles
north of the national park in Carlsbad, New Mexico (pop.
25,000). One of the nicer motor inns there is the **Park Inn**,
on the south edge of town at 3706 National Parks
Highway, (505) 887-2861, with doubles at $48 to $56 a
night. The budget-basic **Lorilodge**, 2019 S. Canal Street,
(505) 887-1171, offers doubles starting at $35.

Nightlife
The big evening attraction at Carlsbad Caverns during the
summer months is the ranger presentation that starts just
before sundown at the visitor center and climaxes with the
dusk flight of a huge cloud of bats from the cave entrance.
The number of bats that migrate up from Mexico for the
warm months to take up residence in Carlsbad Cavern
varies depending on how many insects there are in the
Guadalupe Mountains. There may be as few as 300,000
bats in the cave in a drought year, as many as one million
in a wet year. A million Mexican freetail bats devour more
than ten tons of insects each night.

CARLSBAD CAVERNS TO EL PASO

There are a lot of empty miles between Carlsbad Caverns and El Paso. Break the trip into easy-to-manage segments with a morning canyon hike in Guadalupe Mountains National Park and an afternoon visit to Huecos Tanks State Park.

Suggested Schedule

9:00 a.m.	Leave White's City.
10:00 a.m.	Hike a trail, such as the Smith Spring Trail or a portion of the McKittrick Canyon Trail, in Guadalupe Mountains National Park (see yesterday's Sightseeing Highlights). Pack a picnic lunch.
1:00 p.m.	Drive on.
3:00 p.m.	Explore Huecos Tanks State Park.
5:00 p.m.	Camp at Huecos Tanks or drive to El Paso and check into your accommodations there.

Travel Route: Carlsbad Caverns to El Paso (146 miles)
From White's City, retrace yesterday's route south, enjoying the spectacular descent of the Guadalupe Mountains after you reenter Texas. Stay on US 62/180 all the way to El Paso, a total distance of 146 miles from Carlsbad Caverns. The turnoff to Huecos Tanks State Park is 32 miles from El Paso.

Sightseeing Highlight
▲▲**Huecos Tanks State Park**—This large, fractured volcanic dome has been a West Texas landmark for centuries, partly because of its unique appearance and partly because of the potlike depressions ("tanks") in the rock which capture rain to form the only waterholes around. Indians began coming to Huecos Tanks at least 10,000 years ago, as shown by distinctive Folsom points found here, and if you scramble up the rocks from the picnic ground, you

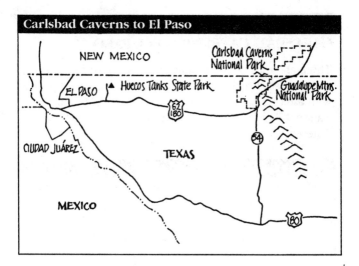

Carlsbad Caverns to El Paso

can locate Indian petroglyphs from Pueblo people who settled here about 1,000 years ago and more recent pictographs painted by Mescalero Apaches as well as caves and rock shelters. Also in the park are the ruins of a stagecoach station established in 1858. The park is open daily from 8:00 a.m. to 10:00 p.m. Admission is $2 per vehicle.

Lodging

El Paso's elegantly restored historic landmark hotel (now a more visible landmark since the addition of a modern 17-story tower in 1986) is the **Camino Real Paso del Norte**, downtown at 101 S. El Paso Street, (915) 534-3024. Built in 1912, this hotel is where Pancho Villa dined and did business with North American arms dealers during the Mexican Revolution. Decor includes crystal chandeliers and a Tiffany stained-glass dome above the lobby, and guest rooms are furnished in Queen Anne style. Room rates are $135.

An outstanding bed and breakfast inn is **Room with a View**, 821 Rim Road, (915) 534-4400. The B&B is situated on a hilltop in an exclusive neighborhood, and the view takes in most of El Paso and Ciudad Juárez as well as a good bit of the Rio Grande, West Texas, and southern New Mexico. The $60 double rate includes a full southwestern-style breakfast. Since there are only four guest rooms (one with a waterbed), reservations are essential.

The highest concentration of budget motels is along North Mesa Drive, off I-10 in the northwest section of the city.

Camping

Huecos Tanks State Historical Park (see Sightseeing Highlights) has a small public campground—only twenty sites, but not often full. Camping here will let you explore the rock maze at leisure. All sites have water and electric hookups and cost $9 per night.

If you should find the campground at Huecos Tanks full, there is a small private RV park called **Desert Oasis** on US 62/180 between the park turnoff and the city. Full hookup sites cost $11 per night for two people, and there is a swimming pool. Several much larger and somewhat costlier private RV parks are situated east of El Paso along I-10 near the Yarbrough and Americas Avenue exits.

Food

Tex-Mex restaurants predominate in El Paso, and the Mexican food there equals any on the far side of the border. An easy one to find is **El Nido**, serving tasty roast goat in a nice atmosphere, located off I-10 at 6932 Gateway East across from the Cielo Vista Mall, 779-9586, open Monday through Saturday from 7:00 a.m. to 8:00 p.m., Sunday from 9:00 a.m. to 6:00 p.m. One of the most offbeat and interesting Mexican fast-food places in town is the **Tortas Grill**, 4190 Mesa (at Executive Center Boulevard), 533-3663. *Tortas*, the house specialty, are Mexican-style submarine sandwiches, served with *licuados* (fruit smoothies). The grill is open Sunday through Thursday from 10:00 a.m. to 1:00 a.m., Friday and Saturday from 10:00 a.m. to 3:30 a.m.

Two good restaurants downtown, both moderate to expensive, are **Dominic's**, 717 E. San Antonio Street, 544-0011, serving creative Italian cuisine Monday through Friday from 11:00 a.m. to 10:00 p.m. and Saturday from 4:00 to 10:00 p.m., and the nouveau-cuisine **Cafe Central**,

1 Texas Court, 545-2233, open Monday through Thursday from 11:00 a.m. to 10:00 p.m., Friday and Saturday from 11:00 a.m. to 10:30 p.m.

Paradoxically, the best restaurants in Ciudad Juárez serve dishes you wouldn't think of as Mexican food. Try Mexican beef, tougher but tastier than American beef because the cattle are not fattened in feedlots, at the moderately priced (upscale for Juárez) **Montana Cattle Company** at Avenida Lincoln 1142 near the ProNaF.

EL PASO AND CIUDAD JUÁREZ

The two cities are one city, founded on the banks of the Rio Grande in 1680, long before the first missionary came to San Antonio. It was a way station on the Camino Real ("Royal Road"), which linked the earliest settlements in New Mexico with Mexico City. More than 150 years later, the United States/Mexican border came up the river and sliced the city in two. Today, the adjoining border cities of El Paso, Texas (pop. 520,000), and Ciudad Juárez, Mexico (population estimates vary—over 1,000,000), comprise a metropolitan area larger than Dallas, with two-thirds of the residents living on the Mexican side of the river. Each of the two cities is the largest border community in its nation, and Ciudad Juárez is the fourth-largest city in Mexico.

Suggested Schedule

8:30 a.m.	Drive to Tigua Pueblo.
9:00 a.m.	See Tigua Pueblo.
10:30 a.m.	Stop at Chamizal National Memorial or the Magoffin Home.
12:00 noon	Visit the U.S. Border Patrol Museum.
1:00 p.m.	Walk across Paso del Norte Bridge to Ciudad Juárez. See the marketplace, the cathedral, and the tourist traps.
Or	Drive across the Cordova Bridge to shop for fine Mexican arts and crafts at ProNaF.
5:00 p.m.	Return to the United States. Drive up Trans Mountain Road for sunset.

Sightseeing Highlights

▲▲**Tigua Indian Pueblo and Ysleta Mission**—The tiny Tigua Pueblo is one of only two Indian reservations in Texas. Like the Alabama-Coushatta people (see Day 4), the Tiguas were not native to Texas but came here by historical accident during the colonial period. In 1680, the Indian pueblos around Santa Fe in northern New Mexico rose up against Spanish settlers and chased them down the Rio

Grande as far as El Paso del Norte (now the city of El Paso), where the Spaniards camped for 11 years before an army came from Mexico City to reclaim New Mexico. When the Spanish fled, they brought with them most of the population of Isleta Pueblo (south of the present-day city of Albuquerque, New Mexico), though history is unclear as to whether the Indians came as slaves or as voluntary refugees. They built the original Ysleta Mission (also called Nuestra Señora del Carmen), which predates any of the Spanish colonial mission churches in San Antonio. Originally on the Mexican side of the Rio Grande, the mission "moved" to the United States side when the river course changed in an early nineteenth-century flood. Near the restored mission, descendants of the Tigua people have reconstructed the old pueblo, Ysleta del Sur, on the original foundations, using some of the old walls. Today the pueblo is a ceremonial and cultural center with a museum and gallery of Pueblo Indian arts and crafts, a restaurant serving traditional dishes such as gorditas and green chile stew, and demonstrations of pottery making, bread baking, and other Pueblo skills.

The mission and pueblo are located 14 miles south of downtown on Old Pueblo Road. From I-10, take either exit 32 (Zaragosa Road) or exit 34 (Avenue of the Americas) and drive south for 2 miles. The pueblo is open daily from 8:00 a.m. to 6:00 p.m. during the summer months, until 5:00 p.m. the rest of the year. Dances are performed on Saturday and Sunday year-round and Wednesday through Friday during the summer months. Call 853-1033 for the current dance and craft demonstration schedules. Admission is $1.50 per adult and $1 per child ages 5 to 12 on days when dances are held, free on other days.

▲**Chamizal National Memorial**—This 55-acre park occupies a tract of land that was claimed by both the United States and Mexico until 1963 in the longest-lasting border dispute in American history. Almost a century ago, the Rio Grande shifted course, isolating the land from Mexico. An international treaty provided that land would belong to one country if the river changed course due to erosion but to the other country if the change was because

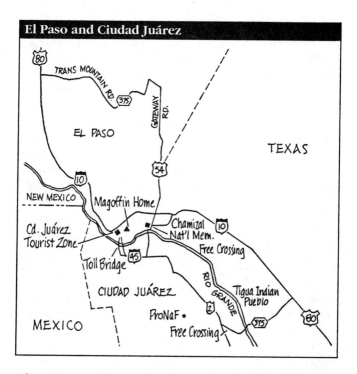

of avulsion; unfortunately, the experts could not agree as to which process had rechanneled the river in this case. Finally, Presidents John F. Kennedy and Adolfo Lopez Mateos broke the deadlock by digging a concrete canal through the center of the Chamizal. The Rio Grande flows through the canal now; the land on the south side of the canal belongs to Mexico, the land on the north to the United States. The treaty that settled the dispute provided that the land on both sides of the canal could only be used for park or recreational purposes. On the United States side, the National Park Service operates a small museum that presents exhibits explaining the complex problems of establishing an international border and a film, *This Most Singular Country,* dramatizing the adventurous story of early surveying expeditions along the Rio Grande. The theater in the park hosts over 180 stage performances each year. Major events include the Siglo de Oro Festival (classical Spanish drama) in March, the Border Jazz Festival on Memorial Day weekend, and the Border Folk Festival (international music and dance) in early October. The park is open daily from 8:00 a.m. to 5:00 p.m. Admission is free. Ticket prices to theater performances vary. For current show information, call 534-6277. Chamizal National Memorial is located at 700 E. Marcial, off Paisano Drive (US 62) near the interchange with Gateway Drive (US 54).

▲**Magoffin Home State Historic Site**—Built in 1875 by import-export merchant James Wiley Magoffin, this historic home is a fine example of the territorial style of architecture that developed in the Southwest with the coming of railroads. It is a synthesis of traditional Spanish adobe building methods with North American architecture and materials. The adobe walls, three feet thick, protect the interior from summer heat and retain the warmth of the fireplaces on cold winter nights. The Greek revival exterior design and Victorian furnishings make for an eclectic but pleasing ambience. The Magoffin Home is located near downtown at 1120 Magoffin Avenue (one-way eastbound, off Mesa Street midway between I-10 and Paisano Drive). Hours are Wednesday through Sunday from 9:00 a.m. to 4:00 p.m., closed Mondays and Tuesdays. Tours of the home are conducted frequently during open hours. Admission is $2 for adults, $1 for children ages 6 to 12.

▲**U.S. Border Patrol Museum**—Everything you'll ever want to know about America's land borders and the adventures of those who guard them is in this one-of-a-kind museum established by the Fraternal Order of Retired Border Patrol Officers. Here you'll learn about one side of the cat-and-mouse game that is played out nightly on the Rio Grande. On display are memorabilia, documents, and photographs tracing the Border Patrol to its Wild West origins in 1924, when border guards on horseback traveled the blistering Chihuahua Desert and the snow-blasted frontier with Canada. (Before 1924, the border with Mexico was open, but there were no paved roads anywhere near here.) Other exhibits show how helicopters, radar, and computers aid modern law enforcement in keeping people out of our country. It may make you proud to be an American, or at least glad not to be a job-hunting Mexican national. The U.S. Border Patrol Museum is in the basement of the Cortez Building at 310 N. Mesa in downtown El Paso. It is open Monday through Friday from 10:00 a.m. to 4:00 p.m., Saturday 9:00 a.m. to 12:00 noon, closed Sundays. Admission is by donation.

▲▲▲**Ciudad Juárez**—It is colorful and loud, touristy and exotic, poverty-stricken by United States standards and one of the most prosperous cities in Mexico. Three bridges cross between El Paso and Ciudad Juárez. If you are driving your vehicle over, you can cross the border on the free Cordova Bridge (take Avenue of the Americas south off I-10, about 16 miles east of downtown El Paso). On the other side, Avenue of the Americas becomes Avenida de las Americas and then Avenida Lincoln (named for its statue of Abraham Lincoln, the only one outside the United States). Lincoln takes you to ProNaF, a modern shopping district where you'll find the FONART (also called Centro Artesanal), a government store displaying and selling quality art and craft items from all over Mexico, open daily from 10:00 a.m. to 7:00 p.m. Nearby is the Museo de Arte y Historia, where exhibits focus on the art of pre-Columbian Mexico, open Tuesday through Sunday from 11:00 a.m. to 7:00 p.m., closed Mondays and Mexican holidays, admission 50 cents for adults, students with ID and children under 12 free. From ProNaF, you can take Avenida 16 de Septiembre west to the downtown area and follow Avenida Juárez north to Paso del Norte Bridge, the busy northbound-only bridge to downtown El Paso.

Remember, you must buy Mexican auto insurance before driving your vehicle to Juárez. It is available from numerous brokers on the approach to each border bridge, typically for about $10 a day. Think of it as an admission charge to Mexico, or leave your vehicle in the United States and walk across the border. From downtown Ciudad Juárez, you can take a taxi to ProNaF and back for the same price as buying auto insurance, and you don't have to drive in crazy Juárez traffic. You can walk over the border from El Paso to Juárez on either Paso del Norte Bridge (Santa Fe Avenue on the U.S. side, Juárez Avenue on the Mexican side) or, four blocks south, Stanton Bridge

(Stanton on the U.S. side, Lerdo on the Mexican side). Pedestrians pay a small toll each way—20 cents on Paso del Norte Bridge, 10 cents on Stanton Bridge. Guarded parking on the United States side of either bridge costs about $2 per day.

In downtown Ciudad Juárez, the tourist zone extends from Paso del Norte Bridge south along Avenida Juárez. Here you'll be cajoled by salespeople from the array of curio shops to purchase all manner of goods from onyx elephants, stuffed armadillos, and factory-produced Mayan sculpture replicas to sombreros, cotton blankets, guitars, and Mexican-made designer jeans. If you have the patience to sort through the tourist junk, you'll find bargains, especially on leather goods such as jackets, boots, saddles, and seatcovers, which sell at a fraction of United States prices. Haggle hard! The tourist zone has plenty of restaurants and nightclubs. Services ranging from prostitution (ubiquitous because of the big U.S. Air Force base to the north) to dentistry (quality work at surprisingly low prices) also help lure norteamericanos across the border.

South of the tourist zone and a block east of Juárez are the landmark Cathedral de Guadalupe Ysleta del Sur and its small neighbor, Nuestra Señora de Guadalupe Mission, the original mission church built here in 1659. Across the square from the cathedral is a public food market where small shops sell fresh produce. (You can't bring fresh fruits or vegetables back to the United States, but the shady cathedral square makes a good picnic spot.)

See "How to Use This Book" for more information on border crossings.

▲**Trans Mountain Road**—For the most spectacular view of El Paso and Ciudad Juárez, take this one-hour drive out around the extreme western tip of Texas. Drive westbound on I-10 for 12 miles from downtown El Paso to exit 6 (Trans Mountain Road) and head east. The paved road over a steep, narrow pass known as Smuggler's Gap (elevation 5,250 feet) takes you to outstanding views overlooking portions of Texas, New Mexico, and Chihuahua, Mexico, as you travel along the sides of rugged mountains and scary cliffs. Completed in 1969, the 10-mile Trans

Mountain Road took over three years to build. You'll pass through a portion of Franklin Mountains State Park and get back into traffic at Gateway Road. Heading south, Gateway will return you to I-10 east of downtown near Chamizal National Monument. Near the Gateway end of Trans Mountain Road, you'll find the Wilderness Park Museum, which has exhibits on ancient Indians of the region (open Tuesday through Sunday from 9:00 to 4:45; free).

ON THE ROAD AGAIN

At the end of this three-week Texas tour, you find yourself at the western extremity of the state, closer to the Pacific Ocean than to the easternmost point on the Texas Gulf Coast. From here, if you are traveling without time limits, you can continue westward to explore other parts of the American Southwest. The Grand Canyon is nearer than Dallas, and Las Vegas, Nevada, is nearer than Houston.

If you are taking a circular trip and wish to return to your Dallas/Fort Worth starting point to close the loop, here are two ways to do it.

Return to Dallas/Fort Worth (direct interstate route— 617 miles)

You can travel from El Paso to the Metroplex in a day, driving for about 11 hours on I-10 and I-20, never leaving the interstate except for hamburgers and gasoline. You might as well drive straight through, because there's not much in the way of points of interest along the interstate route. You'll pass through the twin cities of Odessa and Midland, whose economies are built on oil exploration. Former U.S. president George Bush moved to Midland after World War II, worked there as an oil company executive, and established his credentials as a Texan. The big sightseeing highlight in Midland is the Permian Basin Petroleum Museum, with a large diorama of prehistoric marine life, a re-creation of a 1920s boomtown, and lots of old-fashioned drilling rigs. Take exit 136 from I-20. Open Monday through Saturday from 9:00 a.m. to 5:00 p.m., Sunday 2:00 to 5:00 p.m., admission $3 for adults, $2.50 for seniors, and $1.50 for students ages 6 to 18. Midland is also the new site of the Confederate Air Force Museum. The CAF preserves military aircraft of World War II at various airports around the country and displays a dozen or so in the museum. Open Monday through Saturday from 9:00 a.m. to 5:00 p.m., Sunday from 12:00 noon to 5:00 p.m.; admission $4 for adults, $3 for students and senior citizens, and $2 for children ages 6 to 12.

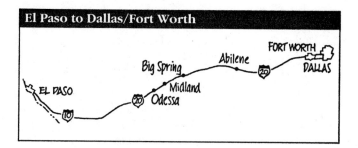

Also along I-20, Big Spring State Recreation Area is a mesa-top park on the southern outskirts of the town of Big Spring. It has a great view and a prairie dog town. The recreation area is open daily from 8:00 a.m. to 8:00 p.m. (until 10:00 p.m. during the summer months). Admission is $2 per vehicle.

Return to Dallas/Fort Worth (scenic route via New Mexico and the Panhandle—900 miles)

My primary 22-day itinerary bypasses the Texas Panhandle completely. The northern reaches of Texas (Panhandle locals refer to it as West Texas and call the region around Big Bend, the Guadalupe Mountains, and El Paso the Trans-Pecos) are a flat, windblown land of dusty-looking farms that depend on well-water irrigation from the dwindling underground reservoir known as the Ogalalla Aquifer. Texas Friendly is spoken with a pronounced regional accent, and residents may tend to stare at you as if to say, "What's a tourist doing way out here?"

But there is one sightseeing highlight in the center of the Panhandle, totally unexpected in the flat, plain landscape, spectacular enough that it would merit inclusion in the main 22-day itinerary if it weren't so far from anyplace else of interest. Palo Duro Canyon State Park preserves a portion of the state's biggest canyon in area and is the largest state park in Texas except for the planned Big Bend Ranch State Park. Palo Duro Canyon is colorful, 400-foot red rock cliffs forming a backdrop for riverside greenery with plenty of picnicking, camping, and swimming areas. The canyon is important in the region's history. The first

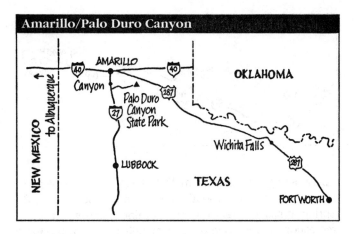

Amarillo/Palo Duro Canyon

rancher in the western half of Texas, Charles Goodnight,
established his homestead here in the 1870s because the
canyon walls were too steep for cattle to climb, providing
natural containment in the days before barbed wire. Ruins
of some old ranch buildings still survive, and a part of the
Texas State Longhorn Herd grazes on the canyon rim.
Before Goodnight homesteaded it, Palo Duro Canyon
provided a labyrinthine hideout for renegade Comanche
Indian bands and Anglo outlaws. The park is open daily
from 8:00 a.m. to 10:00 p.m. Admission is $5 per vehicle,
and campsites cost $10. To get to Palo Duro Canyon, exit
I-40 at Amarillo and drive 16 miles south on I-27 to the
town of Canyon, where there are motels and supermarkets.
From Canyon, follow the park road east for about 16 miles
to the park entrance.

The easiest way to get to the Panhandle from El Paso is
to take I-25 north to Albuquerque, New Mexico, a five-
hour drive, and then travel east to Amarillo on I-40. From
there, four-lane US 287 takes you eventually to the
Dallas/Fort Worth area. If you allow a week for this
segment of the trip, you can take time to explore the many
attractions of the Albuquerque-Santa Fe-Taos region, the
favorite summer vacation and ski trip destination for many
Texans. New Mexico sightseeing is beyond the scope of
this book; you'll find complete information in its companion volume, *2 to 22 Days in the American Southwest.*

INDEX

Other Books from John Muir Publications

Travel Books by Rick Steves

Asia Through the Back Door,
4th ed., 400 pp. $16.95

**Europe 101: History, Art, and
Culture for the Traveler,**
4th ed., 372 pp. $15.95

**Mona Winks: Self-Guided
Tours of Europe's Top
Museums,** 2nd ed., 456 pp.
$16.95

**Rick Steves' Best of the
Baltics and Russia,** 1995
ed. 144 pp. $9.95

Rick Steves' Best of Europe,
1995 ed., 544 pp. $16.95

**Rick Steves' Best of France,
Belgium, and the
Netherlands,** 1995 ed., 240
pp. $12.95

**Rick Steves' Best of
Germany, Austria, and
Switzerland,** 1995 ed., 240
pp. $12.95

**Rick Steves' Best of Great
Britain,** 1995 ed., 192 pp.
$11.95

Rick Steves' Best of Italy,
1995 ed., 208 pp. $11.95

**Rick Steves' Best of
Scandinavia,** 1995 ed., 192
pp. $11.95

**Rick Steves' Best of Spain
and Portugal,** 1995 ed., 192
pp. $11.95

**Rick Steves' Europe Through
the Back Door,** 13th ed.,
480 pp. $17.95

**Rick Steves' French Phrase
Book,** 2nd ed., 112 pp. $4.95

**Rick Steves' German Phrase
Book,** 2nd ed., 112 pp. $4.95

**Rick Steves' Italian Phrase
Book,** 2nd ed., 112 pp. $4.95

**Rick Steves' Spanish and
Portuguese Phrase Book,**
2nd ed., 288 pp. $5.95

**Rick Steves'
French/German/Italian
Phrase Book,** 288 pp. $6.95

A Natural Destination Series

Belize: A Natural Destination,
2nd ed., 304 pp. $16.95

**Costa Rica: A Natural
Destination,** 3rd ed., 400
pp. $17.95

**Guatemala: A Natural
Destination,** 336 pp. $16.95

Undiscovered Islands Series

**Undiscovered Islands of the
Caribbean,** 3rd ed., 264 pp.
$14.95

**Undiscovered Islands of the
Mediterranean,** 2nd ed., 256
pp. $13.95

**Undiscovered Islands of the
U.S. and Canadian West
Coast,** 288 pp. $12.95

For Birding Enthusiasts

**The Birder's Guide to Bed
and Breakfasts: U.S.
and Canada,** 288 pp.
$15.95

**The Visitor's Guide to the
Birds of the Central
National Parks: U.S. and
Canada,** 400 pp. $15.95

**The Visitor's Guide to the
Birds of the Eastern
National Parks: U.S. and
Canada,** 400 pp. $15.95

**The Visitor's Guide to the
Birds of the Rocky
Mountain National Parks:
U.S. and Canada,** 432 pp.
$15.95

Unique Travel Series

Each is 112 pages and $10.95
paperback.

Unique Arizona
Unique California
Unique Colorado
Unique Florida
Unique New England
Unique New Mexico
Unique Texas
Unique Washington

2 to 22 Days Itinerary Planners

**2 to 22 Days in the American
Southwest,** 1995 ed., 192
pp. $11.95

2 to 22 Days in Asia, 192 pp. $10.95

2 to 22 Days in Australia, 192 pp. $10.95

2 to 22 Days in California, 1995 ed., 192 pp. $11.95

2 to 22 Days in Eastern Canada, 1995 ed., 240 pp $12.95

2 to 22 Days in Florida, 1995 ed., 192 pp. $11.95

2 to 22 Days Around the Great Lakes, 1995 ed., 192 pp. $11.95

2 to 22 Days in Hawaii, 1995 ed., 192 pp. $11.95

2 to 22 Days in New England, 1995 ed., 192 pp. $11.95

2 to 22 Days in New Zealand, 192 pp. $10.95

2 to 22 Days in the Pacific Northwest, 1995 ed., 192 pp. $11.95

2 to 22 Days in the Rockies, 1995 ed., 192 pp. $11.95

2 to 22 Days in Texas, 1995 ed., 192 pp. $11.95

2 to 22 Days in Thailand, 192 pp. $10.95

22 Days Around the World, 264 pp. $13.95

Other Terrific Travel Titles

The 100 Best Small Art Towns in America, 224 pp. $12.95

Elderhostels: The Students' Choice, 2nd ed., 304 pp. $15.95

Environmental Vacations: Volunteer Projects to Save the Planet, 2nd ed., 248 pp. $16.95

A Foreign Visitor's Guide to America, 224 pp. $12.95

Great Cities of Eastern Europe, 256 pp. $16.95

Indian America: A Traveler's Companion, 3rd ed., 432 pp. $18.95

Interior Furnishings Southwest, 256 pp. $19.95

Opera! The Guide to Western Europe's Great Houses, 296 pp. $18.95

Paintbrushes and Pistols:

How the Taos Artists Sold the West, 288 pp. $17.95

The People's Guide to Mexico, 9th ed., 608 pp. $18.95

Ranch Vacations: The Complete Guide to Guest and Resort, Fly-Fishing, and Cross-Country Skiing Ranches, 3rd ed., 512 pp. $19.95

The Shopper's Guide to Art and Crafts in the Hawaiian Islands, 272 pp. $13.95

The Shopper's Guide to Mexico, 224 pp. $9.95

Understanding Europeans, 272 pp. $14.95

A Viewer's Guide to Art: A Glossary of Gods, People, and Creatures, 144 pp. $10.95

Watch It Made in the U.S.A.: A Visitor's Guide to the Companies that Make Your Favorite Products, 272 pp. $16.95

Parenting Titles

Being a Father: Family, Work, and Self, 176 pp. $12.95

Preconception: A Woman's Guide to Preparing for Pregnancy and Parenthood, 232 pp. $14.95

Schooling at Home: Parents, Kids, and Learning, 264 pp., $14.95

Teens: A Fresh Look, 240 pp. $14.95

Automotive Titles

The Greaseless Guide to Car Care Confidence, 224 pp. $14.95

How to Keep Your Datsun/Nissan Alive, 544 pp. $21.95

How to Keep Your Subaru Alive, 480 pp. $21.95

How to Keep Your Toyota Pickup Alive, 392 pp. $21.95

How to Keep Your VW Alive, 25th Anniversary ed., 464 pp. spiral bound $25

TITLES FOR YOUNG READERS AGES 8 AND UP

American Origins Series
Each is 48 pages and $12.95 hardcover.
Tracing Our English Roots
Tracing Our French Roots
Tracing Our German Roots
Tracing Our Irish Roots
Tracing Our Italian Roots
Tracing Our Japanese Roots
Tracing Our Jewish Roots
Tracing Our Polish Roots

Bizarre & Beautiful Series
Each is 48 pages, $9.95 paperback, and $14.95 hardcover.
Bizarre & Beautiful Ears
Bizarre & Beautiful Eyes
Bizarre & Beautiful Feelers
Bizarre & Beautiful Noses
Bizarre & Beautiful Tongues

Environmental Titles
Habitats: Where the Wild Things Live, 48 pp. $9.95
The Indian Way: Learning to Communicate with Mother Earth, 114 pp. $9.95
Rads, Ergs, and Cheeseburgers: The Kids' Guide to Energy and the Environment, 108 pp. $13.95
The Kids' Environment Book: What's Awry and Why, 192 pp. $13.95

Extremely Weird Series
Each is 48 pages, $9.95 paperback, and $14.95 hardcover.
Extremely Weird Bats
Extremely Weird Birds
Extremely Weird Endangered Species
Extremely Weird Fishes
Extremely Weird Frogs
Extremely Weird Insects
Extremely Weird Mammals
Extremely Weird Micro Monsters
Extremely Weird Primates
Extremely Weird Reptiles
Extremely Weird Sea Creatures
Extremely Weird Snakes
Extremely Weird Spiders

Kidding Around Travel Series
All are 64 pages and $9.95 paperback, except for *Kidding Around Spain* and *Kidding Around the National Parks of the Southwest*, which are 108 pages and $12.95 paperback.
Kidding Around Atlanta
Kidding Around Boston, 2nd ed.
Kidding Around Chicago, 2nd ed.
Kidding Around the Hawaiian Islands
Kidding Around London
Kidding Around Los Angeles
Kidding Around the National Parks of the Southwest
Kidding Around New York City, 2nd ed.
Kidding Around Paris
Kidding Around Philadelphia
Kidding Around San Diego
Kidding Around San Francisco
Kidding Around Santa Fe
Kidding Around Seattle
Kidding Around Spain
Kidding Around Washington, D.C., 2nd ed.

Kids Explore Series
Written by kids for kids, all are $9.95 paperback.
Kids Explore America's African American Heritage, 128 pp.
Kids Explore the Gifts of Children with Special Needs, 128 pp.
Kids Explore America's Hispanic Heritage, 112 pp.
Kids Explore America's Japanese American Heritage, 144 pp.

Masters of Motion Series
Each is 48 pages and $9.95 paperback.
How to Drive an Indy Race Car
How to Fly a 747
How to Fly the Space Shuttle

Rainbow Warrior Artists Series

Each is 48 pages, $9.95 paperback, and $14.95 hardcover.

Native Artists of Africa
Native Artists of Europe
Native Artists of North America

Rough and Ready Series

Each is 48 pages, $9.95 paperback, and $12.95 hardcover.

Rough and Ready Cowboys
Rough and Ready Homesteaders
Rough and Ready Loggers
Rough and Ready Outlaws and Lawmen
Rough and Ready Prospectors
Rough and Ready Railroaders

X-ray Vision Series

Each is 48 pages and $9.95 paperback.

Looking Inside the Brain
Looking Inside Cartoon Animation
Looking Inside Caves and Caverns
Looking Inside Sports Aerodynamics
Looking Inside Sunken Treasures
Looking Inside Telescopes and the Night Sky

Ordering Information

Please check your local bookstore for our books, or call **1-800-888-7504** to order direct. All orders are shipped via UPS; see chart below to calculate your shipping charge for U.S. destinations. **No post office boxes please; we must have a street address to ensure delivery**. If the book you request is not available, we will hold your check until we can ship it. Foreign orders will be shipped surface rate unless otherwise requested; please enclose $3 for the first item and $1 for each additional item.

For U.S. Orders

Totaling	Add
Up to $15.00	$4.25
$15.01 to $45.00	$5.25
$45.01 to $75.00	$6.25
$75.01 or more	$7.25

Methods of Payment

Check, money order, American Express, MasterCard, or Visa. We cannot be responsible for cash sent through the mail. For credit card orders, include your card number, expiration date, and your signature, or call **1-800-888-7504**. American Express card orders can only be shipped to billing address of cardholder. Sorry, no C.O.D.'s. Residents of sunny New Mexico, add 6.25% tax to total.

Address all orders and inquiries to:

John Muir Publications
P.O. Box 613
Santa Fe, NM 87504
(505) 982-4078
(800) 888-7504